THE PILGRIM'S NEW GUIDE TO THE HOLY LAND

THE PILGRIM'S NEW GUIDE TO THE HOLY LAND

Stephen Doyle, OFM

A Michael Glazier Book
THE LITURGICAL PRESS
Collegeville, Minnesota

ACKNOWLEDGEMENTS

The publisher wishes to acknowledge and thank the following for use of illustrations in this book: The Israel Tourist Office, pages 15, 65, 68 and 121. Carolyn Osiek, R.S.C.J., pages 25, 77, 99 and 147. Jude J. McGeehan, O.F.M., of the Commissariat of the Holy Land page 47 . *The Biblical Archaeology Review*, pages 49, 55, 79, (©Zev Radovan) and 138 (©Werner Braum). The crucifix on page 22 and the stations of the cross on pages 22, 24, 27, 28, 30, 31, 33, 34, 36, 38, 39, 41, 42 and 44 ©Eric Gill.

The publisher also wishes to thank the following copyright holders for the hymns reproduced in this book: World Library Publications, pages 174, 181, 189-192, 194-197, 202-203. Rev. Willard F. Jabusch, page 201. G.I.A. Publications, page 185. Manna Music, Inc., page 184.

A Michael Glazier Book
published by
THE LITURGICAL PRESS

Cover design by Placid Stuckenschneider, O.S.B.

8   9

Library of Congress Cataloging-in-Publication Data

Doyle, Stephen C.
    The pilgrim's new guide to the Holy Land / Stephen Doyle.
        p.   cm.
    Reprint. Originally published: Wilmington, Del. : M. Glazier, c1985.
    "A Michael Glazier book."
    Includes bibliographical references and index.
    ISBN 0-8146-5440-1
    1. Christian shrines—Jerusalem—Guide-books. 2. Christian pilgrims and pilgrimages—Palestine—Guide-books. 3. Jerusalem--Description—Guide-books. 4. Palestine—Description and travel--Guide-books. I. Title.
BX2320.5.P19D69   1990
263'.0425694—dc20
                                                    90-13306
                                                        CIP

CONTENTS

Part III
Holy Places West of Jerusalem

Part IV
Holy Places South of Jerusalem

Part V
Holy Places North of Jerusalem

Appendices

Maps

Hymns

Alleluia! Sing to Jesus
Amazing Grace! How Sweet the Sound
A Mighty Fortress
Angels We Have Heard on High
At the Cross Her Station Keeping
Battle Hymn of the Republic
Children Sing with Voices Gay
The Church's One Foundation
Come Holy Ghost
Crown Him with Many Crowns
Faith of Our Fathers
For All the Saints
God's Blessing Sends Us Forth
Hail Queen of Heaven
The Holy City
Holy, Holy, Holy! Lord God Almighty
How Great Thou Art
I Am the Bread of Life
Let Us Break Bread Together
The Magnificat
Michael Row the Boat Ashore
O Come, All Ye Faithful
O Come, O Come, Emmanuel
O Sacred Head Surrounded
Priestly People
Silent Night
Sing of Mary
The Spirit of God
Swing Low
There Is One Lord
We Three Kings of Orient Are
Were You There?
Whatsoever You Do
Where Charity and Love Prevail
Yes, I Shall Arise

PREFACE

It is obvious from the list at the back of this book that many other books on the Holy Land are available; they contain much detailed information, and are extremely helpful.

This book has its own purpose. It is meant to help a tourist become a pilgrim. Too many have come home from the land of Jesus disappointed. They have been bombarded with more facts than they ever wanted to know. They have been rushed through the shrines so as to spend more time in the gift shops. Even when carrying a Bible they have had no time or opportunity to find the appropriate passages. Much less have they been given time for what must be a major priority of a pilgrimage: prayer.

With this book, a pilgrim can make up for those deficiencies and hopefully transform a hectic tour into a grace-filled pilgrimage.

I have written this book because I have seen the need for it after having led hundreds of pilgrims. It provides the basic information related to each sacred place. This is kept to a minimum because further detailed information is available elsewhere.

What most other books do not have are the spiritual components necessary for a pilgrimage. Included here are the full texts of the Biblical readings, a reflection on the mystery commemorated at each spot, a prayer, and suggested hymns to be sung.

I am most grateful to those who opened up the Bible and its land to me, the Professors of the Pontifical Biblical Institute, Rome. I wish also to express my thanks to the Franciscan Friars of the Custody, who have truly been brothers. As a guest in their land, I ask God's blessings and peace on Arabs and Jews. They have been gracious hosts.

Stephen C. Doyle, O.F.M.

JERUSALEM, JERUSALEM

Important Dates in the History of the Holy City Jerusalem

Circa 1750 BC Abraham, our father in faith makes a mutual defense treaty with Melchizedeck. (Genesis 14:18-20, cf. Hebrews 7)

Circa 1200 The Israelites are unable to occupy Jerusalem when they invade the land flowing with milk and honey. (Judges 1:21)

Circa 1000 David captures the city located on Mount Zion and makes it his capital. This is not the present city of Jerusalem but the small hill at the juncture of the Hinnom and Kidron valleys. Today it is occupied by the Arab village of Silwan. (2 Samuel 5:6ff)

Circa 950 Solomon expands the City of David to include Mount Moriah, where he builds the Temple (1 Kings 5-6). Today it is the site of the Dome of the Rock and the El Aqsa Mosque.

587 Babylonians destroy the city and level the temple, taking the leaders into captivity until 537 when Cyrus the Persian permits them to return. (2 Kings 25)

537ff.	Some of the Jews return from captivity and build a modest temple. (Haggai 1 and 2; Zechariah 8; Isaiah 62; Tobit 13:9-18)
167 - 164	The Syrian, Antiochus Epiphanes IV, defiles the Temple, setting up a statue of himself to be worshipped (Abomination of Desolation). Judas Maccabeus leads revolt and cleanses the temple, relighting the lamps and, thus, initiating the feast of Hanukkah. (1 Maccabees 1-4; Daniel 9:24-27)
1 - 33 AD	Vision of Zechariah: Luke 1:15 Presentation of Jesus: Luke 2:22 Jesus Instructs the teachers: Luke 2:41 Jesus enters Jerusalem, cleanses the temple, preaches and predicts the fall of the Holy City; Luke 19:28 - 21:38
33	Jesus is condemned to death and crucified outside the walls, on the skull-shaped hill called Golgotha. On the third day he rises from the dead. (Luke 22 - 24)
Circa 40-44	Herod Agrippa builds the "Third Wall" which encloses Golgotha, previously outside the city.
70	The city is destroyed by the Romans. (Luke 21:20-24)
132	Second Jewish revolt led by the self-styled messiah Simon bar Cochba is put down; the city is leveled, and the new Roman city of Aelia Capitolina is built. The Jews are forbidden to enter it under pain of death.
326	The Emperor Constantine at the bidding of his mother St. Helena begins construction of the Church of the Holy Sepulchre.
638	The city falls to the Muslims.
688	The Dome of the Rock is begun to commemorate the spot where his followers believe Mohammed ascended into heaven.

1099	The city is taken by the Crusaders who establish the Latin Kingdom of Jerusalem, lasting for almost one hundred years.
1187	The city falls to Saladin, leader of the Seljuk Turks of Asia Minor.
1250	Capture of Egypt by the Mameluke Turks.
1517	Ottoman (Turkish) Empire rules until expelled by the League of Nations for siding with the Germans in World War I.
1918	Great Britain rules under mandate from the League of Nations.
1948	The United Nations resolution calling for the partitioning of Palestine into Arab and Jewish states. Upon the withdrawal of the British, fierce fighting breaks out between Israelis and Arabs and ends with the Holy City on the West Bank under the rule of Jordan.
1967	After the Six Day war, the Old City comes under the control of the Israelis.

The Walls and Gates of the Holy City of Jerusalem

THE WALLS

The walls of Jerusalem have moved and changed as the city has shifted, contracted and expanded over the centuries. Excavations in the City of David, now outside and south of the walled city, have uncovered traces of Jebusite walls dating from the time of Abraham. The present walls, for the most part, date back to only the mid-sixteenth century. A sharp eye will notice a variety in the size and trim of the stone creating different levels and indicating the remains of earlier fortifications. Ascents to the walk on top of the walls are inside the Jaffa Gate and Zion Gate.

THE GATES

Damascus Gate leads out to the road to Damascus, scene the conversion of St. Paul. (Acts 9) It leads into the Suq or bazaar and the Moslem Quarter.

New Gate (1887) leads out to the western part of the new city. Across the street is the monumental Notre Dame of Jerusalem Centre, run by the Vatican. As the French Hospice, it was the scene of some of the heaviest fighting of the 1948 war. The New Gate leads into the Christian Quarter, site of the Church of the Holy Sepulchre and headquarters for the Franciscan Custody of the Holy Land, and the Latin, Greek Catholic and Orthodox Patriarchs.

Jaffa Gate exits westward, toward the cities of Jaffa and Tel Aviv. It is called "The Gate of the Friend" by the Arabs since a pilgrimage to Hebron and the tomb of Abraham, the friend of God, would start from here. Entering the gate, the so-called Citadel Tower of David (the remains of one of Herod's towers) stands on the right and the Christian Quarter lies off to the left. Straight ahead is David Street and the bazaar. The Christian Information Center, which provides information, guidebooks, pilgrimage certificates and reservations for liturgies is just inside Jaffa Gate.

Zion Gate exits to the south and into the area which has come to be called Mount Zion. Here, one may visit the "Tomb of David," the Cenacle (or Upper Room), the Chapel of the Last Supper in the Franciscan Friary, and the Benedictine Dormition Abbey. Below these sites, in the valley to the east, is the Assumptionist Fathers' Church of St. Peter in Gallicantu (of the Cock Crowing), from which can be had a magnificent view of the original Mount Zion or City of David.

The Zion Gate leads into the Armenian Quarter. Near the center of this quarter of the city stands the Cathedral of St. James. The Jewish Quarter may be reached by turning to the right and traveling eastward. The pockmarks in the gate are mute evidence of the violent fighting that has occurred here in recent wars.

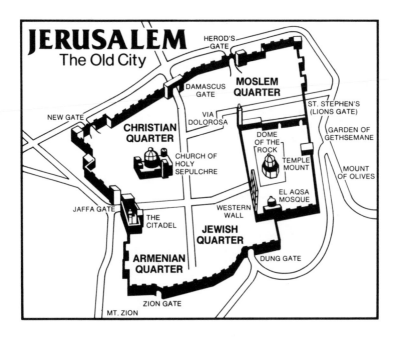

Dung Gate leads out to the ancient City of David, now the Arab village of Silwan, site of recent important archaeological excavations that have been hindered by ultra-orthodox Jews who fear desecration of ancient graves. It leads into the Jewish Quarter, the Synagogue — Plaza facing the Western Wall. From it, one can ascend by ramp to the Temple Mount (Mount Moriah) which, with the Dome of the Rock and El Aqsa Mosque, is an esplanade sacred to the Moslems.

St. Stephen's Gate leads out to the Kidron Valley, the Garden of Gethsemane and the Mount of Olives. It leads into the Crusader church of St. Anne and the beginning of the Via Dolorosa.

Herod's Gate leads out to Arab East Jerusalem and the Rockefeller Museum and into the residential section of the Moslem Quarter. Bearing to the left inside the gate will also bring one to the beginning of the Via Dolorosa.

PART I

HOLY PLACES IN
JERUSALEM

A Pilgrim's Prayer

Lord Jesus Christ, you were a pilgrim in this Holy Land. Now you lead and guide us on our pilgrimage to the heavenly Jerusalem.

As we follow in your steps, we ask the grace to keep our eyes on you. Open our hearts that we may find you not only in ancient stones, but in your people and in each other. Let your words be a fire burning within us. Write your Gospel upon our hearts.

Give us a spirit of prayer lest we return full of facts but not of grace and love. Lord, teach us to pray in the very land where you taught your disciples so that we may say:

Our Father, who art in heaven, hallowed be thy name.
Thy kingdom come, thy will be done on earth as it is in heaven.
Give us this day our daily bread
and forgive us our trespasses
as we forgive those who trespass against us,
And lead us not into temptation, but deliver us from evil.
AMEN

HOLY PLACES IN
JERUSALEM

THE CHURCH OF ST. ANNE

Inside St. Stephen's Gate, on a property facing the temple Mount, is the Church of St. Anne, standing just as it was built by the crusaders. It is in the charge of the White Fathers of Africa. Legend has it that the crypt contains the home of Mary's parents, Joachim and Anne.

Nearby excavations have thrown light on a passage of the Fourth Gospel — Jesus' curing of the sick man at the "pool with five porticoes." Skeptics had contended that there was no such pool. But precisely such a pool was found here and identified as the pool of Bethesda. Since this pool "with five porticoes" provides the setting for Jesus' cure of the sick man, an event which capsulizes the animosity against him and leads to his passion, it can be considered spiritually what it is geographically, the preface to the Via Dolorosa.

John 5:1-15
Cure on a Sabbath Feast.

> Later, on the occasion of a Jewish feast, Jesus went up to Jerusalem. Now in Jerusalem by the Sheep Pool there is a place with the hebrew name Bethesda. Its five porticoes

were crowded with sick people lying there blind, lame or disabled (waiting for the movement of the water). There was one man who had been sick for thirty-eight years. Jesus, who knew he had been sick a long time, said when he saw him lying there, "Do you want to be healed?" "Sir," the sick man answered, "I do not have anyone to plunge me into the pool once the water has been stirred up. By the time I get there, someone else has gone in ahead of me." Jesus said to him, "Stand up! Pick up your mat and walk!" The man was immediately cured; he picked up his mat and began to walk.

The day was a sabbath. Consequently, some of the Jews began telling the man who had been cured, "It is the Sabbath, and you are not allowed to carry that mat around." He explained: "It was the man who cured me who told me, 'Pick up your mat and and walk.'" "This person who told you to pick it up and walk," they asked, "who is he?" The man who had been restored to health had no idea who it was. The crowd in that place was so great that Jesus had been able to slip away.

Later on, Jesus found him in the temple precincts and said to him: "Remember, now, you have been cured. Give up your sins so that something worse may not overtake you." The man went off and informed the Jews that Jesus was the one who had cured him.

Reflection

Suffering can diminish people or make them grow. How sad it is to encounter those who have become whining, petty, and complaining when confronted with illness or the burdens of age. What a joy to come in contact with those whose spirit glows even when they are suffering. What accounts for the difference? Some ask the right question, and some ask the wrong question.

Some ask, "Why is God doing this to me; what did I do to deserve this?" That's the wrong question. It presumes that all suffering is due to personal sin and comes as a punishment from a vindictive God. Such a question presupposes that there is an angry God out there just waiting for us to make a false move.

That is what has been called "ambush theology," and it presents a God with a totally different image than the God Jesus revealed to us.

Such a question is fundamentally wrong, because it has no answer. It can only lead to frustration, pettiness and complaining. Even Jesus did not tell us why there is suffering in the world, or where it comes from.

What Jesus did was this: He helped us to ask the right question. "What can I do with this illness, this suffering?" This question has an answer, an answer that will enable us to grow and to help others. We can do with our suffering what Jesus did with his. We can join it to his and continue his work of saving the world. Because we are one with him, he is willing to consecrate our sufferings as part of his priestly work, if we will embrace it with love.

Jesus did not physically heal everyone he met, as he did this man at the pool. He does not say to everyone, "Rise and walk." But he is always willing to heal. He may begin the healing by helping us to ask the right question.

Prayer

Father, help us to realize that suffering has taken on a whole new dimension since your son embraced the cross. Pour out your blessing on doctors and nurses and all who continue the healing ministry of Jesus. And to all who bear the cross of illness or pain, give a heart filled with love so that the evil of suffering may be transformed into the glory of sacrifice.

This we ask through Christ, Our Lord. Amen.

THE VIA DOLOROSA

The Via Dolorosa or Way of the Cross begins in an area believed to have been once part of the Fortress Antonia, which overlooked the Temple and served as headquarters for the Roman garrison charged with keeping the peace. Opinion is divided on whether Pilate passed judgment on Jesus here or across the city at Herod's Palace, where the Armenian compound is now situated. The authentic place is not important — the following of Jesus is.

On Fridays at 3:00 p.m. the Franciscans lead a procession along the Via Dolorosa. Easy access to this area is gained by entering St. Stephen's Gate. In a newly established park, opposite the Church of St. Anne, the route of the Via Dolorosa is clearly marked on a stone wall.

First Station

If the al-Omariya school is not in session, entrance is permitted to the schoolyard. Otherwise this station can be kept in the courtyard or in one of the beautiful chapels of the Friary of the Flagellation, the Franciscan Biblical School.

On the floor in the rear of the chapel (to the left) are serrated stones of a street either of the time of Jesus or of the Roman city of Aelia Capitolina (135 A.D.).

Jesus is condemned to death

We adore you most Holy Lord Jesus Christ, and we bless you. Because by your holy cross you have redeemed the world.

John 19:1-11

Pilate's next move was to take Jesus and have him scourged. The soldiers then wove a crown of thorns and fixed it on his head, throwing around his shoulders a cloak of royal purple. Repeatedly they came up to him and said, "All hail, king of the Jews!" slapping his face as they did so.

Pilate went out a second time and said to the crowd: "Observe what I do. I am going to bring him out to you to make you realize that I find no case (against him)." When Jesus came out wearing the crown of thorns and the purple cloak, Pilate said to them, "Look at the man!" As soon as the chief priests and the temple guards saw him they shouted, "Crucify him! Crucify him!" Pilate said, "Take him and crucify him yourselves; I find no case against him." "We have our law," the Jews responded, "and according to that law he must die because he made himself God's Son." When Pilate heard this kind of talk, he was more afraid than ever.

Going back into the praetorium, he said to Jesus, "Where do you come from?" Jesus would not give him any answer. "Do you refuse to speak to me?" Pilate asked him. "Do you not know that I have the power to release you and the power to crucify you?" Jesus answered:

"You would have no power over me whatever unless it were given you from above. That is why he who handed me over to you is guilty of the greater sin."

John 3:17-19

God did not send the Son into the world to condemn the world, but that the world might be saved through him. Whoever believes in him avoids condemnation, but whoever does not believe is already condemned for not believing in the name of God's only Son.

The judgement of condemnation is this: the light came into the world, but men loved darkness rather than light because their deeds were wicked.

Prayer

Lord Jesus, ours is the guilt, yours is the judgement; ours is the crime, yours is the punishment. Forgive us for what we have done. We are blind and weak, but we are the people that you came to save. Enlighten and strengthen us with your saving grace. As we begin to walk the sorrowful way with you, we pray that you may walk with us all the days of our life. Grant this, Jesus, Saving Lord. Amen.

Hymn

O Sacred Head, surrounded By crown of piercing thorn.
O bleeding Head, so wounded Reviled and put to scorn.
Our sins have marred the glory of thy most holy face.
Yet angel hosts adore thee, and tremble as they gaze.
(page 189)

Second Station

The second station may be prayed underneath the "Ecce Homo Arch" or in the archaeological excavations beneath the convent of the Sisters of Sion who will graciously provide a guide. The arch, the other half of which forms part of the beautiful sanctuary of the church, probably dates from shortly after the time of Jesus. The stone floor in the base-

*"The second station may be prayed
underneath the 'Ecce Homo Arch'..."*

ment may be the courtyard of the fortress Antonia, where
the soldiers who mocked Jesus left the scratchings of their
games.

Jesus embraces the cross

*We adore You most Holy Lord Jesus Christ, and we
bless You. Because by Your Holy Cross You have
redeemed the world.*

John 19:12-17

> After this, Pilate was eager to release him, but the Jews
> shouted, "If you free this man you are no 'Friend of
> Caesar.' Anyone who makes himself a king becomes
> Caesar's rival." Pilate heard what they were saying, then
> brought Jesus outside and took a seat on a judge's bench
> at the place called the Stone Pavement — Gabbatha in

Hebrew. (It was the Preparation Day for Passover, and the hour was about noon.) He said to the Jews, "Look at your king!" At this they shouted, "Away with Him! Away with him! Crucify him!" "What!" Pilate exclaimed. "Shall I crucify your king?" The chief priests replied, "We have no king but Caesar." In the end Pilate handed Jesus over to be crucified.

Jesus was led away, and carrying the cross by himself, went out to what is called the Place of the Skull (in Hebrew Golgotha).

John 10:11, 17-18

I am the good shepherd; the good shepherd lays down his life for the sheep.

The Father loves me for this: that I lay down my life to take it up again.

No one takes it from me; I lay it down freely. I have power to lay it down, and I have power to take it up again. This command I received from my Father.

Prayer

Lord Jesus you embraced your cross, but we so frequently shy away from the crosses you hold out to us. You have shown us that suffering without love is demeaning. But suffering embraced with love can become saving sacrifice. By your wounds we are healed, and in union with you, by our wounds, we can heal others. Fill our hearts with that selfless love by which you became our Saviour.
Grant this, Jesus, Saving Lord. Amen.

Hymn

The Lord of every nation Was hung upon a tree.
His death was our salvation, Our sins, his agony.
O Jesus, by thy passion, thy life in us increase.
Thy death for us did fashion Our pardon and our peace.
(page 189)

Third Station

At the end of the street turn left and immediately notice the paving stones from the time of Jesus that have recently been raised from the original level several feet below. On the left is the entrance to the courtyard of the Polish Hospice and the Armenian Catholic Church inside which the third station may be prayed.

Jesus falls the first time

We adore you most Holy Lord Jesus Christ, and we bless You. Because by Your Holy Cross You have redeemed the world.

Psalm 43

Do me justice, O God, and fight my fight against a faithless people; from the deceitful and impious man rescue me.

For you, O God, are my strength. Why do you keep me so far away? Why must I go about in mourning, with the enemy oppressing me?

Send forth your light and your fidelity; they shall lead me on and bring me to your holy mountain, to your dwelling-place. Then will I go in to the altar of God, the God of my gladness and joy; Then will I give you thanks upon the harp, O God, my God!

Why are you so downcast, O my soul? Why do you sigh within me? Hope in God! For I shall again be thanking him, in the presence of my savior and my God.

Prayer

Lord Jesus, you "emptied yourself and took the form of a slave." Forgive us for exalting ourselves. You embraced our

humanity in all its weakness and failings. Give us the wis-
dom to see our own humanity as a gift that can strengthen
your brothers and sisters when they fall.
  Grant this, Jesus, Saving Lord. Amen.

Hymn

Yes, I shall arise and return to my Father!
To you, O Lord, I lift up my soul;
In you, O my God, I place all my trust!   (page 203)

Fourth Station

This station, marked IV, is a short distance to the left
when leaving the courtyard. The sounds and commotion of
the street, though reminiscent of the atmosphere which
Jesus himself encountered, may be diminished by staying
the courtyard of the Armenian Catholic Church, or in the
Church itself.

Jesus meets Mary, his mother

We adore You most Holy Lord Jesus Christ, and we bless
You. Because by Your Holy Cross You have redeemed
the world.

Lamentations 2:13, 15, 18, 19

  To what can I liken or compare you, O daughter
Jerusalem? What example can I show you for your com-
fort, virgin daughter Zion? For great as the sea is your
downfall; who can heal you?
  All who pass by clap their hands at you; They hiss and
wag their heads over daughter Jerusalem: Is this the
all-beautiful city, the joy of the whole earth?"
  Cry out to the Lord; moan, O daughter Zion! Let your

tears flow like a torrent day and night; Let there be no respite for you, no repose for your eyes.

Rise up, shrill in the night, at the beginning of every watch; Pour out your heart like water in the presence of the Lord; Lift up your hands to him for the lives of your little ones (who faint from hunger at the corner of every street).

Luke 2:28-35

Simeon took him in his arms and blessed God in these words: "Now, Master, you can dismiss your servant in peace; you have fulfilled your word. For my eyes have witnessed your saving deed displayed for all the peoples to see: A revealing light to the Gentiles, the glory of your people Israel."

The child's father and mother were marveling at what was being said about him. Simeon blessed them and said to Mary his mother: "This child is destined to be the downfall and the rise of many in Israel, a sign that will be opposed and you yourself shall be pierced with a sword — so that the thoughts of many hearts may be laid bare."

Prayer

Lord Jesus, from the cross you gave us your Mother to be our own. Her love for you and her fidelity to the will of your Father challenge us. She bore you in her womb and brought forth the Light into the world of darkness. May we, who follow her example, as your disciples, bear you in our hearts and bring you forth into the darkness of our weary world.
Grant this, Jesus, Saving Lord. Amen.

Hymn

At the cross her station keeping, Stood the mournful Mother weeping, Close to Jesus to the last.

Through her heart, his sorrow sharing, All his bitter anguish bearing, Now at length the sword has passed. (page 175)

Fifth Station

This station is prayed at the corner where the Via Dolorosa turns and begins to go uphill.

Simon from Cyrene helps Jesus

We adore You most Holy Lord Jesus Christ, and we bless You. Because by Your Holy Cross You have redeemed the world.

Luke 23:26

> As they led him away, they laid hold of one Simon the Cyrenean who was coming in from the fields. They put a crossbeam on Simon's shoulder for him to carry along behind Jesus.

Luke 9:23-26

> Jesus said to all: "Whoever wishes to be my follower must deny his very self, take up his cross each day, and follow in my steps. Whoever would save his life will lose it, and whoever loses his life for my sake will save it. What profit does he show who gains the whole world and destroys himself in the process? If a man is ashamed of me and my doctrine, the Son of Man will be ashamed of him when he comes in his glory and that of his Father and his holy angels."

Prayer

Lord Jesus, we like to think that if we were there, we would have come to your aid. But how often have we seen you in the least of your brethren and either turned our backs or stood apart as a guilty bystander? Forgive us, for we have seen wounds, and did not recognize them as yours. Forgive

us, for we have seen crosses burdening bent backs and did
not perceive that the face was yours.
Grant this, Jesus, Saving Lord. Amen.

Hymn
*Whatsoever you do to the least of my children, that you do
unto me. (page 201)*

Sixth Station

Continuing up the Via Dolorosa, on the left, one comes to
the Chapel of the Sixth Station. If the door is not open, a
Little Sister of Jesus next door in the Ikon shop will open it.
The Ikon of Jesus' face on the sanctuary wall vividly brings
to life this ancient legend.

Veronica wipes the face of Jesus

*We adore You most Holy Lord Jesus Christ, and we
bless You. Because by Your Holy Cross You have
redeemed the world.*

2 Corinthians 4:5-18

It is not ourselves we preach but Christ Jesus as Lord,
and ourselves as your servants for Jesus' sake. For God,
who said, "Let light shine out of darkness" has shone in
our hearts, that we in turn might make known the glory of
God shining on the face of Christ.

This treasure we possess in earthern vessels to make it
clear that its surpassing power comes from God and not
from us. We are afflicted in every way possible, but we are
not crushed: full of doubts, we never despair. We are
persecuted but never abandoned; we are struck down but
never destroyed. Continually we carry about in our

bodies the dying of Jesus, so that in our bodies the life of Jesus may also be revealed.

While we live we are constantly being delivered to death for Jesus' sake, so that the life of Jesus may be revealed in our mortal flesh. Death is at work in us, but life in you. We have that spirit of faith of which the Scripture says, "Because I believed, I spoke out." We believe and so we speak, knowing that he who raised up the Lord Jesus will raise us up along with Jesus and place both us and you in his presence. Indeed, everything is ordered to your benefit, so that the grace bestowed in abundance may bring greater glory to God because they who give thanks are many.

We do not lose heart, because our inner being is renewed each day even though our body is being destroyed at the same time. The present burden of our trial is light enough, and earns for us an eternal weight of glory beyond all comparison. We do not fix our gaze on what is seen but on what is unseen. What is seen is transitory; what is unseen lasts forever.

Prayer

Lord Jesus, as you passed along your way, the enmity must have been hard to bear. But the indifference of those who just did not care must have hurt you terribly. How many passed by and did not so much as notice you, because they were busy. Help us to stop running. Make us cease from our busy-ness. Make us hear the words: "Be still and know that I am God" (Ps. 46:10).

Grant this, Jesus, Saving Lord. Amen.

Hymn

Whatsoever you do to the least of my children, that you do unto me. (page 201)

Seventh Station

At the end of the street, directly in front of you, before turning, is a base of a pillar from the ancient city, and a door marked with a crusader's cross. The cross-street is the Suq, so that this is one of the busiest crossways of the old city. The crowd will usually be heavy and pushing, as it would have been in Jesus' day; falling here, one could almost be trampled underfoot.

Jesus falls the second time

We adore You most Holy Lord Jesus Christ, and we bless You. Because by Your Holy Cross You have redeemed the world.

Psalm 40:2-4, 14-18

I have waited, waited for the Lord, and he stooped toward me and heard my cry. He drew me out of the pit of destruction, out of the mud of the swamp; He set my feet upon a crag; he made firm my steps. And he put a new song into my mouth, a hymn to our God. Many shall look on in awe and trust in the Lord.

Deign, O Lord, to rescue me; O Lord, make haste to help me. Let all be put to shame and confusion who seek to snatch away my life. Let them be turned back in disgrace who desire my ruin. Let them be dismayed in their shame who say to me, "Aha, aha!" But may all who seek you exult and be glad in you, And may those who love your salvation say ever, "The Lord be glorified." Though I am afflicted and poor, yet the Lord thinks of me. You are my help and my deliverer; O my God, hold not back!

Prayer

Lord Jesus, your burden is heavy but even though you stumble, you rise again to do your Father's will. So often we get discouraged and seem crushed by the burdens of life. That is when we think we have to carry them ourselves, and forget that you said: "Come to me all you who labor and are heavily burdened and take my yoke upon you, for my yoke is sweet and my burden is light." Strengthen us that when we fall we may clasp your hand and rise.

Grant this, Jesus, Saving Lord. Amen.

Hymn

Yes, I shall arise and return to my Father!
Look down on me, have mercy on me, O Lord;
Forgive me my sins, behold all my grief. (page 203)

Eighth Station

As one leaves the seventh station, one is actually going out the gate of the city wall as it was in the time of Jesus. Thus Calvary and the Sepulchre are both outside the wall of 33 A.D. which ran along here. Turning right, out the Suq, at the seventh station, ascend Aqabat el Khanga to find the eighth station. It is marked on the left by a stone cross in the wall of an Orthodox church.

Jesus meets the daughters of Jerusalem

We adore you most holy Lord Jesus Christ, and we bless you Because by your holy cross you have redeemed the world.

Luke 23:27-31

A great crowd of people followed him, including women who beat their breasts and lamented over him.

Jesus turned to them and said: "Daughters of Jerusalem, do not weep for me. Weep for yourselves and for your children. The days are coming when they will say, 'Happy are the sterile, the wombs that never nursed.' Then they will begin saying to the mountains, 'Fall on us,' and to the hills, 'Cover us.' If they do these things in the green wood, what will happen in the dry?'"

Lamentations 3:49-57

My eyes flow without ceasing, there is no respite,
Till the Lord from heaven looks down and sees.
My eyes torment my soul at the sight of all the
    daughters of my city.
Those who were my enemies without cause
    hunted me down like a bird;
They struck me down alive in the pit,
    and sealed me in with a stone.
The waters flowed over my head,
    and I said, "I am lost!"
I called upon your name, O Lord, from the bottom of the pit:
You heard me call, "Let not your ear be deaf
    to my cry for help!"
You came to my aid when I called to you;
    you said, "Have no fear!"

Prayer

Lord Jesus, in your admonition to these women, you allude to the coming destruction of the city brought down upon the heads of those who sought to bring liberation by violence. They are the dry wood. How terrible that you, the green wood, who sought to bring about change through gentleness and love should suffer their same fate of execution. Strengthen us that we may also be willing to suffer persecution for righteousness sake.

Grant this, Jesus, Saving Lord. Amen.

Hymn

Whatsoever you do to the least of my children, that you do unto me. (page 201)

Ninth Station

If we were medieval pilgrims making the stations, we would be able to go straight from here to the entrance of the Holy Sepulchre. The construction of centuries prevents this, so that we must now retrace our steps, turning right in the Suq. After a short walk, a large staircase appears on the right. Go up these stairs and proceed around to where there is a pillar in the doorway entrance. The ninth station may be prayed here, or one may enter onto the roof of the Chapel of St. Helena where the Ethiopian Monks live. They will graciously permit the station to be celebrated in their chapel (an offering should be given). After the station you can descend into the courtyard of the Basilica. Otherwise, if the station is prayed at the pillar by the entranceway, you must retrace your path; down the staircase into the Suq, and keep bearing to the right, until arrival at the courtyard of the Basilica.

Jesus falls the third time

We adore You most Holy Lord, Jesus Christ, and we bless You. Because by Your Holy Cross You have redeemed the world.

Isaiah 53

Who would believe what we have heard? To whom has the arm of the Lord been revealed? He grew up like a sapling before him, like a shoot from the parched earth; There was in him no stately bearing to make us look at him, nor appearance that would attract us to him. He was spurned and avoided by men, a man of suffering, accustomed to infirmity, One of those from whom men hide their faces, spurned, and we held him in no esteem.

Yet it was our infirmities that he bore, our sufferings that he endured, While we thought of him as stricken, as one smitten by God and afflicted. But he was pierced for our offenses, crushed for our sins; Upon him was the chastisement that makes us whole, by his stripes we were healed. We had all gone astray like sheep, each following his own way; But the Lord laid upon him the guilt of us all.

Though he was harshly treated, he submitted and opened not his mouth; Like a lamb led to the slaughter or a sheep before the shearers — he was silent and opened not his mouth. Oppressed and condemned, he was taken away, and who would have thought any more of his destiny? When he was cut off from the land of the living, and smitten for the sin of his people, A grave was assigned him among the wicked and a burial place with evildoers, Though he had done no wrong nor spoken any falsehood. (But the Lord was pleased to crush him in infirmity.)

If he gives his life as an offering for sin, he shall see his descendants in a long life, and the will of the Lord shall be accomplished through him. Because of his affliction he shall see the light in fullness of days; Through his suffering, my servant shall justify many, and their guilt he shall bear. Therefore I will give him his portion among the great and he shall divide the spoils with the mighty.

Because he surrendered himself to death and was counted among the wicked; And he shall take away the sins of many, and win pardon for their offenses.

Prayer

Lord Jesus, you bow low beneath the cross, but never toss it aside. Your soul is troubled now, but you do not flee from your hour when the grain of wheat must fall into the ground to bear much fruit. Help us that we too may not shy away from the difficulties of life, but face them with love and obedience as you did.

Grant this, Jesus, Saving Lord. Amen.

Hymn

Amazing grace! How sweet the sound, That saved a soul like me! I once was lost but now am found, Was blind but now I see. (page 171)

Tenth Station

This station may be prayed either in the courtyard of the Basilica, on the outside staircase which leads to the closed-off crusader entrance to Calvary, or inside at the foot of the internal staircase, or at the top of the staircase, on Calvary itself. The decision will be based more on numbers than on piety.

Jesus is stripped of his garments

We adore You most Holy Lord Jesus Christ, and we bless You. Because by Your Holy Cross You have redeemed the world.

John 19:23-24

The soldiers took his garments and divided among them four ways, one for each soldier. There was also his tunic, but this tunic was woven in one piece from top to bottom and had no seam. They said to each other, we should not tear it. Let us throw dice to see who gets it. (The purpose of this was to have the scripture fulfilled: They divided my garments among them and for my clothing they cast lots.

Lamentations 3:16-26

He has broken my teeth with gravel, pressed my face in the dust; My soul is deprived of peace, I have forgotten what happiness is; I tell myself my future is lost, all that I hoped for from the Lord.

The thoughts of my homeless poverty are wormwood and gall; Remembering them over and over leaves my soul downcast within me. but I will call this to mind, as my reason to have hope:

The favors of the Lord are not exhausted, his mercies are not spent; They are renewed each morning, so great is his faithfulness.

My portion is the Lord, says my soul; therefore will I hope in him.

Good is the Lord to one who waits for him, to the soul that seeks him; It is good to hope in silence for the saving help of the Lord.

Prayer

Lord Jesus, though you were by nature God, you did not think divine glory something to be clung to. You emptied yourself. For our sakes you made yourself poor, though you were rich, so that we might be enriched by your poverty. Let nothing lord it over our lives, so that only you may be Lord.

Grant this, Jesus, Saving Lord. Amen.

Hymn

Through many dangers, toils, and snares, I have already come; 'Tis grace hath brought me safe thus far, and grace will lead me home. (page 171)

Eleventh Station

Immediately inside the door of the Basilica is a staircase which actually is the ascent of the hill of Calvary. There is another staircase immediately to the right around the corner. The top of Calvary, like the garments of Jesus, is divided. To the right is the Latin altar of the Nailing to the Cross. To the side of it is another Latin altar of Our Lady of Sorrows. To the left is the Greek Orthodox Chapel of the Crucifixion.

Jesus is nailed to the cross

We adore You most Holy Lord Jesus Christ, and we bless You. Because by Your Holy Cross You have redeemed the world.

John 19:18-22

There they crucified him, and two others with him: one on either side, Jesus in the middle. Pilate had an inscription placed on the cross which read,

Jesus the Nazorean
the King of the Jews

This inscription, in Hebrew, Latin and Greek, was read by many of the Jews, since the place where Jesus was crucified was near the city. The chief priests of the Jews tried to tell Pilate, "You should not have written, 'The king of the Jews.' instead, 'This man claimed to be King of the Jews.'" Pilate answered, "What I have written, I have written."

John 15:9-13

As the Father has loved me, so I have loved you. Live on in my love. You will live in my love if you keep my commandments, even as I have kept my Father's commandments, and live in his love. All this I tell you that my joy may be yours and your joy may be complete. This is my commandment: love one another as I have loved you. There is no greater love than this: to lay down one's life for one's friends.

Prayer

Lord Jesus, you have manifested the greatest love one can have: to lay down our life for others. You did not hold back from giving, while so often all that we can think of is grabbing. Forgive our selfishness, correct our self-centeredness. Show us how to stretch out our arms, like yours, in an embrace of love.

Grant this, Jesus, Saving Lord. Amen.

Hymn

Were you there when they nailed him to the tree?
Were you there when they nailed him to the tree?
Oh! Sometimes it causes me to tremble, tremble, tremble.
Were you there when they nailed him to the tree?
(page 200)

Twelfth Station

The spot of the death of our Saviour Jesus can be venerated by getting on one's knees beneath the Greek Orthodox altar. The opening marks the present top of the stone mound (outside the walls in the time of Jesus) which was called the Hill of the Skull or Calvary. Pious legend placed here the tomb of Adam, hence many crucifixes showed a skull beneath the figure of Jesus. Actually the formation got its name from the fact that sides of the mound had been quarried and from a certain perspective it suggested the outline of a skull.

Jesus dies upon the cross

We adore You most holy Lord Jesus Christ, and we bless You. Because by Your Holy Cross You have redeemed the world.

Luke 23:34a, 35-46

Jesus said, "Father forgive them; they do not know what they are doing."

The people stood there watching, and the leaders kept jeering at him, saying, "He saved others; let him save himself if he is the Messiah of God, the chosen one." The soldiers also made fun of him, coming forward to offer him their sour wine and saying, "If you are the king of the Jews, save yourself."

There was an inscription over his head: "This is the King of the Jews."

One of the criminals hanging in crucifixion blasphemed him: "Aren't you the Messiah? Then save yourself and us." But the other one rebuked him: "Have you no fear of God, seeing you are under the same sentence? We deserve it, after all. We are only paying the price for

what we've done, but this man has done nothing wrong."
He then said, "Jesus, remember me when you enter upon
your reign." And Jesus replied, "I assure you: this day
you will be with me in paradise."

It was now around midday, and darkness came over
the whole land until mid-afternoon with an eclipse of the
sun. The curtain in the sanctuary was torn in two. Jesus
uttered a loud cry and said, "Father into your hands I
commend my spirit."

After he said this, he expired.

Prayer

*Lord Jesus, thank you for the love that knew no limits.
"We were once alienated from you. We nourished hostility
in our hearts because of our evil deeds. But now, you have
achieved reconciliation for us in your mortal body, by
dying, so as to present us to God, holy, free of reproach and
blame" (Col. 1:21-22).*

*Make us worthy of your gift of life through the cross.
Grant this, Jesus, Saving Lord. Amen.*

Hymn

*Were you there when they crucified my Lord?
Were you there when they crucified my Lord?
Oh! Sometimes it causes me to tremble, tremble, tremble.
Were you there when they crucified my Lord? (page 200)*

Thirteenth Station

This station may be prayed either in front of the gem-
encrusted image of the Mother of Sorrows on top of Calvary, or having carefully descended the narrow staircase
(sideways is safest), at the red marble stone of anointing
near the Basilica entrance. The stone only goes back to the

19th century. However, the Body of Jesus would have been taken to near this point and prepared for burial.

Jesus is taken down from the cross

We adore You most holy Lord Jesus Christ, and we bless You. Because by Your Holy Cross You have redeemed the world.

John 19:31-40

Since it was the Preparation Day the Jews did not want to have the bodies left on the cross during the sabbath, for that sabbath was a solemn feast day. They asked Pilate that the legs be broken and the bodies be taken away. Accordingly, the soldiers came and broke the legs of the men crucified with Jesus, first of the one, then of the other. When they came to Jesus and saw that he was already dead, they did not break his legs. One of the soldiers thrust a lance into his side, and immediately blood and water flowed out. (This testimony has been given by an eyewitness, and his testimony is true. He tells what he knows is true, so that you may believe.)

These events took place for the fulfillment of Scripture: "Break none of his bones."

There is still another Scripture passage which says: "They shall look on him whom they have pierced."

Afterward, Joseph of Arimathea, a disciple of Jesus (although a secret one for fear of the Jews), asked Pilate's permission to remove Jesus' body. Pilate granted it, so they came and took the body away. Nicodemus (the man who had first come to Jesus at night) likewise came, bringing a mixture of myrrh and aloes which weighed about a hundred pounds. They took Jesus' body, and in accordance with Jewish burial custom bound it up in wrappings of cloth with perfumed oils.

Prayer
Lord Jesus, you have told us "You will grieve for a time, but your grief will be turned into joy... You are sad for a

time, but I shall see you again, and then your hearts will rejoice, with a joy no one can take from you." We truly rejoice, for you have kept your promise. You are with us. Never again shall we be alone. Give us the strength to bear all of our sorrows and losses while your presence turns them to joy. This we ask, Jesus, Saving Lord. Amen.

Hymn

Were you there when they laid him in the tomb?
Were you there when they laid him in the tomb?
Oh! Sometimes it causes me to tremble, tremble, tremble.
Were you there when they laid him in the tomb?
(page 200)

Fourteenth Station

Under the rotunda of the basilica is the edicule of the sepulchre. Originally, a cave in a small hillside, today it stands independently. The surrounding terrain was cleared away by Constantine in order to build the Basilica. The tomb consisted of an outer chamber and an inner burial chamber. The outer one is designated as the Chapel of the Angel who proclaimed the first good news of Easter Sunday. The second contains a slab covered by a piece of marble, where the body of Jesus lay from Good Friday until Easter Sunday. The sad and ugly little structure will be disappointing. But it is Jesus Christ's resurrection and not man's construction that we celebrate.

Jesus is buried and rises to life

We adore You Lord Jesus Christ, and we bless You. Because by Your Holy Cross You have redeemed the world.

Luke 23:50-24:7

There was a man named Joseph, an upright and holy member of the Sanhedrin, who had not been associated with their plan or their action. He was from Arimathea, a Jewish town, and he looked expectantly for the reign of God. This man approached Pilate with a request for Jesus' body. He took it down, wrapped it in fine linen, and laid it in a tomb hewn out of the rock, in which no one had yet been buried.

That was the Day of Preparation, and the sabbath was about to begin. The women who had come with him from Galilee followed along behind. They saw the tomb and how his body was buried. Then they went home to prepare spices and perfumes. They observed the sabbath as a day of rest, in accordance with the law.

On the first day of the week, at dawn, the women came to the tomb bringing the spices they had prepared. They found the stone rolled back from the tomb; but when they entered the tomb, they did not find the body of the Lord Jesus.

While they were still at a loss over what to think of this, two men in dazzling garments stood beside them. Terrified, the women bowed to the ground. The men said to them:

"Why do you search for the Living One among the dead? He is not here; he has been raised up. Remember what he said to you while he was still in Galilee — that the Son of Man must be delivered into the hands of sinful men, and be crucified, and on the third day rise again."

Prayer

Lord Jesus, we are Easter Christians, and alleluia is our song. You are the light that came into darkness, and the darkness was not able to overcome it. From death you arose to newness of life. In our baptism we died and rose with you. Help us to show forth the light of the resurrection to all and proclaim with every word and deed: Christ is risen. He is truly risen.

This we ask, Jesus, Risen Lord. Amen.

Hymn

I am the bread of life. He who comes to me shall not hunger.
He who believes in me shall not thirst. No one can come
to me unless the Father draw him.

And I will raise him up, and I will raise him up,
And I will raise him up on the last day. (page 185)

THE HOLY SEPULCHRE

33 A.D.   Jesus dies on a knoll outside the walls of Jerusalem. Quarrying had given the site the outline of a skull (Golgotha). The Body of Jesus is taken from the cross and buried in a cave in a nearby rise in the ground.

c. 40-44 A.D.   Herod Agrippa increases the size of Jerusalem by erecting the "Third Wall," thus enclosing the area of Calvary and the tomb inside the city.

70 A.D.   The Holy City is leveled by Titus.

135 A.D.   The Roman city of Aelia Capitolina is built on the ruins. The area of the Death and Resurrection of Jesus becomes part of the Roman Forum.

335 A.D.   Emperor Constantine, son of St. Helena, builds a complex including a Basilica to include Calvary and a rotunda over the Sepulchre. To do this, he levels off the sides of Calvary so that it becomes a balcony. Also, he clears the hill away from around the cave of the tomb.

The Church of the Holy Sepulcher.

1099 A.D.   The Basilica, as it now stands, was completed by the Crusaders, incorporating elements of the previous edifices.

1959 A.D.   After fires and earthquakes, the restoration of the Basilica is begun.

As one enters the Church of the Holy Sepulchre, immediately ahead is the stone of the anointing, a nineteenth century addition commemorating the embalming of Jesus' body with spices. The wall behind the stone encloses the area of the Greek Orthodox, as one can detect from the multitude of Ikons. To the right of the stone of anointing are the stairs that bring one to the top of Mount Calvary, with its Latin altar of the Nailing to the Cross, and Greek altar of the Crucifixion.

Turning left from the stone of anointing, one sees a cage-like structure commemorating the women who came and stood at a distance from the cross. ". . . the women who had accompanied him from Galilee were standing at a distance watching everything" (Lk 23:49).

Behind it can be seen the beautiful mosaic of the Armenians, which is at the entrance to their chapel. To the right, under the cupola, is the little building which covers the Holy Sepulchre — found empty on Easter Sunday, for the Lord is truly Risen. The marble slab in the second chamber covers the spot where Jesus' body lay. Most of the original rock of the cave was cleared away by Constantine to build the church. The rest has been covered over with the present structure, which hopefully will one day be removed as the restoration work progresses. Meanwhile the actual stone of the tomb can be touched at the rear where a Coptic monk will allow you access on your knees.

On the other side of the tomb is the area of the Latin Catholics. (Access to the Holy Sepulchre for liturgy, and the number of candles each may burn there, is rigidly determined for the different rites by a "status quo" based on

A woman kneeling at the stone of anointing.

ancient claims and disputes at the spot where the Prince of Peace rose from the dead.)

The beautiful renovations in this area, which is in the care of the Franciscans, include a magnificent new organ. On the organ loft is a bas-relief of the events associated with the Resurrection. Opposite is the altar commemorating Jesus' apparition to Mary Magdalene on Easter Sunday. The splendid sculpture, along with the bas-relief and the Stations of the Cross in the chapel, are the work of Fr. Andrea Martini, O.F.M., of Rome.

John 20:11-18

> Mary stood weeping beside the tomb. Even as she wept, she stooped to peer inside, and there she saw two angels in dazzling robes. One was seated at the head, and the other at the foot of the place where Jesus' body had lain. "Woman," they asked her, "Why are you weeping?" She answered them, "Because the Lord has been taken away, and I do not know where they have put him." She had no sooner said this when she turned around and caught sight of Jesus standing there. But she did not recognize him. "Woman," he asked her, "Why are you weeping? Who is it that you are looking for?" She supposed he was the gardener, so she said: "Sir, if you are the one who carried him off, tell me where you have laid him, and I will take him away." Jesus said to her, "Mary." She turned to him and said, "Rabouni" (which means teacher). Jesus then said, "Do not cling to me, for I have not yet ascended to the Father. Rather, go to my brothers and tell them, I am ascending to my Father and your Father, to my God and your God." Mary Magdalene went to the disciples. "I have seen the Lord," she proclaimed.

The large double door ahead opens to the beautiful Latin Chapel of the Blessed Sacrament where the Eucharist is reserved. A piece of an ancient pillar there is thought to be from the one to which Jesus was tied while being scourged.

Whatever the validity of that claim, it cannot be doubted that this is an oasis of peace and good taste in contrast to the cacophany and confusion of the basilica. It is an ideal spot to pray St. Paul's meditation on the meaning of Christ:

> In the name of the encouragement you owe me in Christ, in the name of the solace that love can give, of fellowship in spirit, compassion, and pity, I beg you: make my joy complete by your unanimity, possessing the one love, united in spirit and ideals. Never act out of rivalry or conceit; rather, let all parties think humbly of others as superior to themselves, each of you looking to others' interests rather than their own.

> Your attitude must be that of Christ.

Though he was in the form of God,
  he did not deem equality with God
  something to be grasped at.
Rather, he emptied himself
  and took the form of a slave,
  being born in the likeness of men.
He was known to be of human estate,
  and it was thus that he humbled himself,
  obediently accepting even death,
  death on a cross!
Because of this,
  God highly exalted him
  and bestowed on him the name
  above every other name,
So that at Jesus' name
  every knee must bend in the heavens, on the earth,
  and under the earth,
  and every tongue proclaim
  to the glory of God the Father:
  JESUS CHRIST IS LORD!

                              (Philippians 2:1-11)

Reflection

A visit to this basilica, holiest spot in the world, can be disappointing. The scandal of the divisions in the church, the body of Christ, is nowhere more apparent than here.

Yet it also shows that Jesus was not afraid to embrace and walk among our seared and scarred humanity. Here he rose from the dead to "free those who through fear of death had been slaves their whole life long" (Heb 2:15). Here the power of risen life is offered to all. From here he challenges his followers to live as proof of his resurrection.

Prayer

God the Father of Our Lord Jesus Christ, Father of glory, grant us a spirit of wisdom and insight to know you clearly. Enlighten our innermost vision so that we may know the great hope to which you have called us, the wealth of your glorious heritage to be distributed among the members of the church, and the immeasurable scope of your power in us who believe. It is the very same power you showed in raising Christ from the dead.

Grant this through Jesus, Our Risen Lord. Amen. (Based on Eph. 1:17 ff.)

Hymns

I Am the Bread of Life (page 185)
Crown Him with Many Crowns (page 178)
Alleluia Sing to Jesus (page 172)

•

Outside the door of the chapel is the sacristy where one may see the sword of the Crusade leader, Godfrey de Bouillon.

The next major spot of interest is reached by keeping the wall of the church to your left and the wall of the Greek sanctuary to your right. Behind the sanctuary, stairs lead to the Armenian chapel. On the stairwell walls are the crosses carved over the centuries by pilgrims. A further descent leads to the cistern, carved out of the rock, in which St. Helena is thought to have discovered the cross of Jesus.

Ascending to the floor of the basilica again, we come on the left to a glass through which can be seen the *rock of Calvary*. A larger portion can be seen around the corner, under the balcony of Calvary. This is the Chapel of Adam. The fissures in the rock, resulting from earthquakes, show why it was abandoned as a quarry.

On coming out into the courtyard once again, one has the evocative experience of emerging from the darkness of the tomb into the brilliant Jerusalem sunshine.

NOTE ON THE GARDEN TOMB

Outside the Damascus Gate on Nablus Road is a lovely garden containing a tomb. It was "discovered" a hundred years ago by an English General (Gordon). The claim that it is Calvary owes more to wishful thinking than to any sense of history, archaeology or tradition. Nevertheless, it can give the idea of what the tomb of Jesus was like better than the Holy Sepulchre, and it is a beautiful, quiet spot for prayer and meditation.

ST. STEPHEN'S BASILICA
THE ECOLE BIBLIQUE

After the Garden Tomb, the next entrance (ring bell) leads into the Church of St. Stephen. The place of the saint's martyrdom is disputed. The Orthodox Church outside of St. Stephen's Gate is the other alleged spot where he shed his blood.

Acts 7:54-60

> Stephen, filled with the Holy Spirit, looked to the sky
> above, and saw the glory of God, and Jesus standing at
> God's right hand.... The onlookers were shouting
> aloud, holding their hands over their ears as they did so.
> Then they rushed at him as one man, dragged him out of
> the city and began to stone him. The witnesses meanwhile
> were piling their cloaks at the feet of a young man named
> Saul. As Stephen was being stoned, he could be heard
> praying: "Lord Jesus, receive my spirit." He fell to his
> knees and cried out in loud voice, "Lord Jesus, do not
> hold this sin against them." And with that, he died.

On the same property is the renowned Ecole Biblique et
Archaeologie Francaise of the Dominicans. The names of
its scholars, Lagrange, Vincent, de Vaux, Benoit, and
Murphy-O'Connor — to mention just a few — are   known
for their contribution to the fields of Biblical and archaeological studies. The widely-used and justly popular Jerusalem Bible originated here.

MOUNT ZION

THE CENACLE
The area that is today designated as Mount Zion is outside the walls, beyond the war-scarred Zion Gate. In times
past it was inside the city walls (cf. The Model of Jerusalem
in 68 A.D. at the Holy Land Hotel. See p. 67).

Two walled compounds immediately outside the gate
enclose the properties of the Armenian Orthodox and of the
Franciscans. The Armenians (whose Cathedral of St. James
is inside the wall of the city) recently excavated their property and uncovered ruins from the time of Jesus that are
thought by some to be the remains of the house of the high
priest.

The Franciscan property is recognizable by the Crusad-

The Cenacle or Upper Room

er's or Holy Land Cross on the iron gates. Ring bell for admittance. Inside is a lovely garden with a fish pond. Ascend the stairs to the newly renovated chapel. The chunk glass window below the bronze figure of the Holy Spirit is just yards away from the actual Cenacle or Upper Room, which the Franciscans possessed until 1552. Since the Cenacle may be used for public prayer services only on Holy Thursday and Pentecost, this chapel is an ideal place to meditate on the mysteries of Christ the Lord which took place in the Upper Room. The magnificent bronzes of the dove, the Last Supper (the host in Jesus' hands is the tabernacle), and Mary are the work of Fr. Andrea Martini, O.F.M.

To reach the actual Cenacle, leave the gate of the Franciscan garden and keep bearing left. A sign proclaiming "House of Prayer for All People" marks the entrance to a rabbinical school. At the top of the stairway to the left is the room that leads into the Upper Room. The Moslem prayer

niche in the center, indicating the direction of Mecca,
alludes to its former use as a mosque. However, the carving,
of the pelican piercing her breast to feed her young, on the
capital of the small pillar, proclaims another tradition. It is
the symbol of the Eucharist and indicates the ancient Christian veneration of this spot as the cite of the institution of the
Eucharist. It is reminiscent of the magnificent basilica that
was built in the fifth century and covered much of Mount
Zion.

John 17:20-26
Last Words

"I do not pray for them alone. I pray also for those who
will believe in me through their word, that all may be one
as you, Father, are in me, and I in you; I pray that they
may be (one) in us, that the world may believe that you
sent me. I have given them the glory you gave me that
they may be one, as we are one — I living in them, you
living in me — that their unity may be complete. So shall
the world know that you sent me.

Father, all those you gave me I would have in my
company where I am, to see this glory of mine which is
your gift to me, because of the love you bore me before
the world began. Just Father, the world has not known
you, but I have known you; and these men have known
that you sent me. To them I have revealed your name, and
I will continue to reveal it so that your love for me may
live in them, and I may live in them."

Matthew 26:26-30
The Last Supper

The Holy Eucharist. During the meal Jesus took
bread, blessed it, broke it, and gave it to his disciples.
"Take this and eat it," he said, "this is my body." Then he
took a cup, gave thanks and gave it to them. "All of you
must drink from it," he said, "for this is my blood, the

blood of the covenant, to be poured out in behalf of many for the forgiveness of sins. I tell you, I will not drink this fruit of the vine from now until the day when I drink it new with you in my Father's reign." Then, after singing songs of praise, they walked out to the Mount of Olives.

John 20:19-28
The Resurrection

Appearance to the Disciples. On the evening of that first day of the week, even though the disciples had locked the doors of the place where they were for fear of the Jews, Jesus came and stood before them. "Peace be with you," he said. When he had said this, he showed them his hands and his side. At the sight of the Lord the disciples rejoiced. "Peace be with you," he said again.

"As the Father has sent me,
so I send you."

Then he breathed on them and said:

"Receive the Holy Spirit.
If you forgive men's sins,
they are forgiven them;
if you hold them bound,
they are held bound."

Appearance to Thomas. It happened that one of the Twelve, Thomas (the name means "Twin"), was absent when Jesus came. The other disciples kept telling him: "We have seen the Lord!" His answer was, "I will never believe it without probing the nailprints in his hands, without putting my finger in the nailmarks and my hand into his side."

A week later, the disciples were once more in the room, and this time Thomas was with them. Despite the locked doors, Jesus came and stood before them. "Peace be with you," he said; then, to Thomas: "Take your finger and examine my hands. Put your hand into my side. Do not persist in your unbelief, but believe!" Thomas said in response, "My Lord and my God!"

Reflection

In this room, the greatest promises that ears have ever heard were made — and kept. Here Jesus spoke his last words. Here he promised that if we abide in him, we would bear much fruit. And then he fulfilled the promise by giving us the means to abide in him: "This is my body; this is my blood."

In this room he promised that although he was leaving us, he would not leave us orphans. "And I will pray to the Father, and he will give you another Counselor, to be with you forever, even the Spirit of truth, whom the world cannot receive, because it neither sees him nor knows him" (John 14:16-17). That promise he fulfilled in this room: "And there appeared to them, tongues as of fire . . . and they were all filled with the Holy Spirit" (Acts 2:3-4).

Here he promised: "Peace I leave with you." On the third day he returned to fulfill it: "Peace be with you. As the Father has sent me, even so, I send you . . . If you forgive the sins of any, they are forgiven; if you retain the sins of any, they are retained" (Jn 20:21,23).

Here, Jesus prayed for us. "I do not pray for these only, but also for those who believe in me through their word" (Jn 17:2). That is ourselves!

The room is empty, but because of the promises made and kept here, our hearts, lives and spirits are full. We are living answers to Jesus' prayer. Our sins are forgiven, the Holy Spirit is with us, and we are strengthened by the Body and Blood of Jesus.

Prayer

Almighty God, you revealed yourself to your people as Yahweh: I am who am present to you. We rejoice in this hallowed room that you are present to us in your Son, Jesus. We praise you that on this spot he left us his presence in his Body and Blood. We praise you that he has fulfilled the promises made here; the Holy Spirit abides in us. May we

never think we are alone again. We ask this in Jesus' name.
Amen.

Hymns

Come Holy Ghost (page 180)
Where Charity and Love Prevail (page 202)
Let Us Break Bread Together (page 186)
Priestly People (page 190)

THE DORMITIAN ABBEY

Upon emergence from the Cenacle turn right and then left to arrive at the Benedictine Abbey commemorating the "sleeping" of Mary, the Mother of the Lord. The event is also commemorated at the underground Orthodox Church in the Garden of Gethsemane and in Ephesus. This basilica was built by the German Benedictines at the turn of the century. An offshoot of this community is the Weston Priory in Vermont.

The church suffered heavy damage during the wars of 1948 and 1967, but has recently been restored. The grandeur of the upper church is in marked contrast to the peaceful serenity of the crypt. Here the statue of Mary in repose is surrounded by mosaics of great biblical women.

1 Corinthians 15:51-55

Now I am going to tell you a mystery. Not all of us shall fall asleep, but all of us are to be changed — in an instant, in the twinkling of an eye, at the sound of the last trumpet. The trumpet will sound and the dead will be raised incorruptible, and we shall be changed. This corruptible body must be clothed with incorruptibility, this mortal body with immortality. When the corruptible frame takes on incorruptibility and the mortal immortality, then will the saying of Scripture be fulfilled: "Death is swallowed up in victory." "O death, where is your victory? O death, where is your sting?"

Hymns
For All the Saints (page 208)
Hail Queen of Heaven (page 183)

TOMB OF DAVID

The so-called "Tomb of David" is now reached by going all the way around the Franciscan property, keeping the parking lot on the left. It is actually in the lower room, directly beneath the Cenacle. The legend locating the tomb here is of comparatively recent origin. King David, the Messiah of the Lord, was actually buried in the old City of David, down the hill, opposite the Temple Mount.

Psalm of David 110:1-4

The Lord said to my Lord: "Sit at my right hand till I make your enemies your footstool. The scepter of your power the Lord will stretch forth from Zion: "Rule in the midst of your enemies. Yours is princely power in the day of your birth, in holy splendor; before the daystar, like the dew, I have begotten you.

"The Lord has sworn and he will not repent: You are a priest forever according to the Order of Melchizedek."

Acts 2:29-33

"Brothers, I can speak confidently to you about our father David. He died and was buried, and his grave is in our midst to this day. He was a prophet and knew that God had sworn to him that one of his descendants would sit upon his throne. He said that he was not abandoned to the nether world, nor did his body undergo corruption, thus proclaiming before hand the resurrection of the Messiah. This is the Jesus God has raised up, and we are his witnesses. Exalted at God's right hand, he first received the promised Holy Spirit from the Father, then poured this Spirit out on us. This is what you now see and hear."

ST. PETER IN GALLICANTU

The church below Mount Zion, overlooking the ancient City of David, is the church of "St. Peter Where the Cock Crowed." Excellent guides are generally available. The doors on the sides of the sanctuary of the upper church lead on to a balcony with a splendid view of the original Zion at the juncture of the Jerusalem valleys. To the left of the church is the stone staircase leading down to the Kidron valley which Jesus likely trod on Holy Thursday night on his way to the Garden of Gethsemane.

John 18:1

> "After this discourse, Jesus went out with his disciples across the Kidron Valley."

Excavations beneath the property have uncovered what may have been the quarters of the high priest where Jesus was denied by Peter, mocked, scourged, and spent the night in prison. If so, he was lowered into the unused cistern, which has been cut open so that now one may enter by means of a staircase. Crosses on the walls indicate the early veneration of the site by pilgrims.

Luke: 22:31-34

> Simon, Simon! Remember that Satan has asked for you, to sift you like wheat. But I have prayed for you that your faith may never fail. You in turn must strengthen your brothers." "Lord," he said to him, "at your side I am prepared to face imprisonment and death itself." Jesus replied, "I tell you, Peter, the cock will not crow today until you have three times denied that you know me."

Luke 22:54-62

> They led him away under arrest and brought him to the house of high priest, while Peter followed at a distance. Later they lighted a fire in the middle of the courtyard and were sitting beside it, and Peter sat among them. A

servant girl saw him sitting in the light of the fire. She gazed at him intently, then said, "This man was with him." He denied the fact, saying, "Woman, I do not know him." A little while later someone else saw him and said, "You are one of them too." But Peter said, "No, sir, not I!" About an hour after that another spoke more insistently: "This man was certainly with him, for he is a Galilean." Peter responded, "My friend, I do not know what you are talking about." At the very moment he was saying this, a cock crowed. The Lord turned around and looked at Peter, and Peter remembered the word that the Lord had spoken to him. "Before the cock crows today you will deny me three times." He went out and wept bitterly.

Psalm 88

O Lord, my God, by day I cry out; at night I clamor in your presence. Let my prayer come before you; incline your ear to my call for help, For my soul is surfeited with troubles and my life draws near to the nether world.

I am numbered with those who go down into the pit; I am a man without strength. My couch is among the dead, like the slain who lie in the grave, whom you remember no longer and who are cut off from your care.

You have plunged me into the bottom of the pit, into the dark abyss. Upon me your wrath lies heavy, and with all your billows you overwhelm me.

You have taken my friends away from me; you have made me an abomination to them; I am imprisoned, and I cannot escape.

My eyes have grown dim through affliction; daily I call upon you, O Lord; to you I stretch out my hands. Will you work wonders for the dead? Will the shades arise to give you thanks? Do they declare your kindness in the grave, your faithfulness among those who have perished? Are your wonders made known in the darkness or your justice in the land of oblivion?

But I, O Lord, cry out to you; with my morning prayer I wait upon you. Why, O Lord, do you reject me; why hide from me your face? I am afflicted and in agony from my youth; I am dazed with the burden of your dread. Your furies have swept over me; your terrors have cut me off. They encompass me like water all the day; On all sides they close in upon me. Companion and neighbor you have taken away from me, my only friend is darkness.

Reflection

In darkness, loneliness and isolation Jesus spends his last night among us. His captors do not know that they have plunged the light of the world into the darkness. The God who said, "Let there be light" is abandoned to the darkness of night in a black prison pit. Here is love beyond telling. Here is giving beyond imagining. Abandoned by all, he will still stretch out his arms to draw all of us to himself. The light has come into the darkness, and the darkness will not overpower it. With God, all things are possible.

Prayer

Lord Jesus, in your prison we lift up to you all who have been unjustly deprived of their human rights and dignity. Like you, they suffer for justice' sake. May they be blessed and be given the gift of freedom. You came to proclaim liberty to prisoners and captives. Pour out your light and love upon all who are in prisons, jails and detention camps. And Lord, enlighten us that we may use our freedom to continue the redemption that you desire for everyone. We ask this Jesus, Saving Lord, Amen.

THE WESTERN WALL AND THE TEMPLE MOUNT

This plateau was begun by Solomon and continued by Herod to level off Mt. Moriah, making a suitable esplanade for the first and second temples. The Western Wall with its lower courses of stones, some weighing as much as twenty tons, was and is part of the retaining wall of that plateau. It is highly venerated as the only remaining vestige of the temple destroyed during the Roman Siege in 70 A.D. Access to it was regained by the Jews in the 1967 war. The whole area is considered to be a synagogue, and is the site of weddings and bar mitzvahs. Prayerful petitions are inserted between the stones.

Upon climbing the ramp which gives access to the Temple Mount, one is met by a sign forbidding entry. Erected by Orthodox Jews, this is intended to discourage any Jew from entering the area and so possibly stepping on the spot of the ancient Holy of Holies, which only the High Priest could enter once a year on the Day of Atonement. Its exact location is disputed.

The area is the site of the Dome of the Rock and the El Aqsa Mosque. The former is named from the rock which it encloses. It was probably the base of the altar of sacrifice which stood in front of the temple. Originally a threshing floor purchased by David, it is also venerated as the site where Abraham was told to offer his son, Isaac. The Moslems revere it as the site from which Mohammed ascended to heaven.

The El Aqsa Mosque, ("Distant" in Arabic) received its name as the most distant mosque from Mecca when it was built. Both were constructed in the seventh century. The whole area is considered a sacred sanctuary.

Luke 2:22-39

When the day came to purify them according to the law of Moses, the couple brought him up to Jerusalem so that he could be presented to the Lord, for it is written in the law of the Lord, "Every firstborn male shall be consecrated to the Lord." They came to offer sacrifice, "a pair of turtledoves or two young pigeons," in accord with the dictate in the law of the Lord.

There lived in Jerusalem at the time a certain man named Simeon. He was just and pious, and awaited the

The Western or Wailing Wall at Sabbath.

consolation of Israel, and the Holy Spirit was upon him. It was revealed to him by the Holy Spirit that he would not experience death until he had seen the Anointed of the Lord. He came to the temple now, inspired by the Spirit and when the parents brought in the child Jesus to perform for him the customary ritual of the law, he took him in his arms and blessed God in these worlds:

> "Now, Master, you can dismiss your
>   servant in peace;
> you have fulfilled your word.
> For my eyes have witnessed your saving deed
> displayed for all the peoples to see:
> A revealing light to the Gentiles,
> the glory of your people Israel."

The child's father and mother were marveling at what was being said about him. Simeon blessed them and said to Mary his Mother: "This child is destined to be the downfall and the rise of many in Israel, a sign that will be opposed — and you yourself shall be pierced with a sword — that the thoughts of many hearts may be laid bare."

There was also a certain prophetess, Anna by name, daughter of Phanuel of the tribe of Asher. She had seen many days, having lived seven years with her husband after her marriage and then as a widow until she was eighty-four. She was constantly in the temple, worshipping day and night in fasting and prayer. Coming on the scene at this moment, she gave thanks to God and talked about the child to all who looked forward to the deliverance of Jerusalem.

When the pair had fulfilled all the prescriptions of the law of the Lord, they returned to Galilee and their own town of Nazareth. The child grew in size and strength, filled with wisdom, and the grace of God was upon him.

Luke 2:42-51

His parents used to go every year to Jerusalem for the feast of Passover, and when he was twelve they went up for the celebration as was their custom. As they were returning at the end of the feast, the child Jesus remained behind unknown to his parents. Thinking he was in the party, they continued their journey for a day, looking for him among their relatives and acquaintances.

Not finding him, they returned to Jerusalem in search of him. On the third day they came upon him in the temple sitting in the midst of the teachers, listening to them and asking them questions. All who heard him were amazed at his intelligence and his answers.

When his parents saw him they were astonished, and his mother said to him: "Son, why have you done this to us? You see that your father and I have been searching for you in sorrow." He said to them: "Why did you search for me? Did you not know I had to be in my Father's house?" But they did not grasp what he said to them.

John 2:13-23

As the Jewish Passover was near, Jesus went up to Jerusalem. In the temple precincts he came upon people engaged in selling oxen, sheep and doves, and others seated changing coins. He made a (kind of) whip of cords and drove sheep and oxen alike out of the temple area, and knocked over the money-changers' tables, spilling their coins. He told those who were selling doves: "Get them out of here! Stop turning my Father's house into a market-place!" His disciples recalled the words of Scripture: "Zeal for your house consumes me."

At this the Jews responded, "What sign can you show us authorizing you to do these things?" "Destroy this temple," was Jesus' answer, "and in three days I will raise it up." They retorted, "This temple took forty-six years to build, and you are going to raise it up in three days!" Actually he was talking about the temple of his body. Only after Jesus had been raised from the dead did his disciples recall that he had said this, and come to believe the Scripture and the word he had spoken.

While he was in Jerusalem during the Passover festival, many believed in his name, for they could see the signs he was performing. For his part, Jesus would not trust himself to them because he knew them all. He needed no one to give him testimony about human nature. He was well aware of what was in man's heart.

Hymn

The Holy City   (page 197)

MODEL OF JERUSALEM

In the garden of the Holy Land Hotel is a model of Jerusalem built on a scale of 1/50. It shows the Holy City as it was two years before its destruction in 70 A.D. It is constantly being changed and revised, on the basis of the most recent archaeological discoveries. The third wall, or the one closest to the entrance gate, is the only thing of major importance that was added after the time of Jesus. A guided visit is most rewarding.

YAD VASHEM MEMORIAL

To a people who felt that they were doomed to annihilation in the Babylonian Exile, Yahweh promised ... "I will give in my house and within my walls a monument (Hebrew *yad* = hand) and a name (Hebrew: *shem*). Better than sons and daughters, an eternal imperishable name will I give them." (Is 56:5) This memorial to the Holocaust of 1939-45 is named from that Isaiah text. It should be a spot of veneration and remembrance on every pilgrimage.

The Memorial Chamber of
Yad Vashem

PART II

HOLY PLACES EAST
OF JERUSALEM

HOLY PLACES
EAST OF JERUSALEM

THE MOUNT OF OLIVES

MOSQUE OF THE ASCENSION
The biblical text is not clear as to where the Ascension took place (cf. Mt 28:16; Lk 24:50). The Moslem custodians of the mosque on the Mount of Olives show no such diffidence. For a fee, they allow the pilgrim to see the rock with the footprint of Jesus!

PATER NOSTER CHURCH
This area was a favorite spot for the Master to bring his disciples. The Carmelite cloister of the Pater Noster Church commemorates Jesus' great gift of the Our Father. Ceramic plaques proclaim it in a multitude of languages. A cave beneath the sanctuary of the uncompleted church is an ideal spot to pray as Jesus taught us to pray.

Luke 11:1-13

> One day he was praying in a certain place. When he had finished, one of his disciples asked him, "Lord, teach us to pray, as John taught his disciples." He said to them, "When you pray, say:

'Father,
hallowed be your name,
your kingdom come.
Give us each day our daily bread.
Forgive us our sins
for we too forgive all who do us wrong;
and subject us not to the trial.'

Jesus said to them: "If one of you knows someone who comes to him in the middle of the night and says to him, 'Friend, lend me three loaves, for a friend of mine has come in from a journey and I have nothing to offer him;' and he from inside should reply, 'Leave me alone. The door is shut now and my children and I are in bed. I cannot get up to look after your needs' — I tell you even though he does not get up and take care of the man because of friendship, he will do so because of his persistence, and give him as much as he needs.

"So, I say to you, Ask and you shall receive; seek and you shall find; knock and it shall be opened to you.

"For whoever asks, receives; whoever seeks, finds; whoever knocks, is admitted. What father among you will give his son a snake if he asks for a fish, or hand him a scorpion if he asks for an egg? If you, with all your sins, know how to give your children good things, how much more will the heavenly Father give the Holy Spirit to those who ask him."

Matthew 6:9-15

"In your prayer do not rattle on like the pagans. They think they will win a hearing by the sheer multiplication of words. Do not imitate them. Your Father knows what you need before you ask him. This is how you are to pray:
'Our Father in heaven,
hallowed be your name,
your kingdom come,
your will be done
on earth as it is in heaven.

Give us today our daily bread,
and forgive us the wrong we have done
as we forgive those who wrong us.
Subject us not to the trial
but deliver us from the evil one.' "

PANORAMA OF JERUSALEM

Across from the Intercontinental Hotel, past the camels and sellers of maps, flutes and bookmarks, is a small amphitheatre with a panoramic view of Jerusalem, across the Kidron Valley. The graves on both sides are of those who desired to be first in line for the last judgment scheduled to take place in the valley of Jehosephat (Joel 4:2 and 12). According to Jewish belief, this will be when the Messiah comes and enters the Temple area. In the wall of the Temple Mount can be seen the sealed-up, double Golden Gate (Beautiful Gate) through which he will pass.

The southeast corner of the retaining wall of the Temple Mount is high above the Kidron Valley. It has been called the pinnacle of the Temple.

Matthew 4:5-7

Next the devil took him to the holy city, set him on the parapet of the temple, and said, "If you are the Son of God throw yourself down. Scripture has it: 'He will bid his angels take care of you; with their hands they will support you that you may never stumble on a stone.'" Jesus answered him, "Scripture also has it: 'You shall not put the Lord your God to the test.'"

Matthew 24:1-2

Jesus left the temple precincts then, and his disciples came up and pointed out to him the buildings of the temple area. His comment was: "Do you see all these buildings? I assure you, not one stone will be left on another — it will all be torn down."

Matthew 26:31-46

"When the Son of Man comes in his glory, escorted by all the angels of heaven, he will sit upon his royal throne, and all the nations will be assembled before him. Then he will separate them into two groups, as a shepherd separates sheep from goats. The sheep he will place on his right hand, the goats on his left. The king will say to those on his right: 'Come. You have my Father's blessing! Inherit the kingdom prepared for you from the creation of the world. For I was hungry and you gave me food. I was thirsty and you gave me drink. I was a stranger and you welcomed me, naked and you clothed me. I was ill and you comforted me, in prison and you came to visit me.' Then the just will ask him: 'Lord, when did we see you hungry and feed you or see you thirsty and give you drink? When did we welcome you away from home or clothe you in your nakedness? When did we visit you when you were ill or in prison?' The king will answer them: 'I assure you, as often as you did it for one of my least brothers, you did it for me.'

"Then he will say to those on his left: 'Out of my sight, you condemned, into that everlasting fire prepared for the devil and his angels! I was hungry and you gave me no food, I was thirsty and you gave me no drink. I was away from home and you gave me no welcome, naked and you gave me no clothing. I was ill and in prison and you did not come to comfort me.' Then they in turn will ask: 'Lord, when did we see you hungry or thirsty or away from home or naked or ill or in prison and not attend you in your needs?'

"He will answer them: 'I assure you, as often as you neglected to do it to one of these least ones, you neglected to do it to me.' These will go off to eternal punishment and the just to eternal life."

Now when Jesus had finished all these discourses, he declared to his disciples, "You know that in two days' time it will be Passover, and that the Son of Man is to be handed over to be crucified."

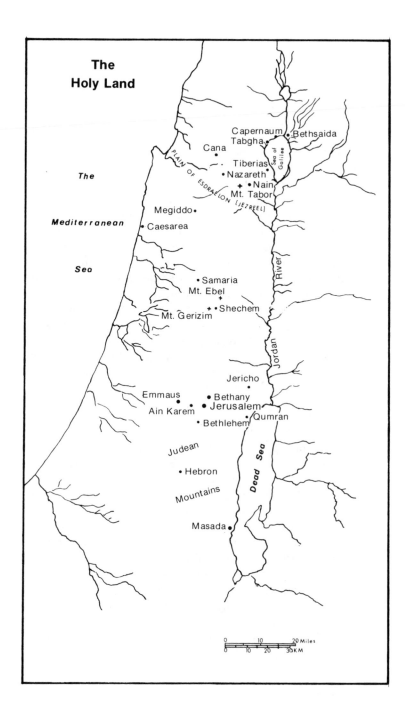

The Holy Land

The

Mediterranean

Sea

PLAIN OF ESDRAELON (JEZREEL)

Capernaum
Tabgha
• Bethsaida
Cana
Tiberias
Sea of Galilee
• Nazareth
+ • Nain
Mt. Tabor

Megiddo •
• Caesarea

• Samaria
Mt. Ebel
+
Mt. Gerizim
+ • Shechem

Jordan River

Jericho
Emmaus
• Bethany
Ain Karem
• Jerusalem
• Bethlehem
Qumran

Judean

• Hebron

Mountains

Dead Sea

Masada •

0   10   20 Miles
0 10 20 30 KM

Acts 3:1-10

Once, when Peter and John were going up to the temple for prayer at three o'clock, a man crippled from birth was being carried in. They would bring him every day and put him at the temple gate called "The Beautiful" to beg from the people as they entered. When he saw Peter and John on their way in, he begged them for an alms. Peter fixed his gaze on the man, so did John. "Look at us!" Peter said. The cripple gave them his whole attention, hoping to get something. Then, Peter said: "I have neither silver nor gold, but what I have I give you! In the name of Jesus Christ the Nazorean, walk!" Then Peter took him by the right hand and pulled him up. Immediately the beggar's feet and ankles became strong; he jumped up, stood for a moment, then began to walk around. He went into the temple with them — walking, jumping about, and praising God. When the people saw him moving and giving praise to God, they recognized him as that beggar who used to sit at the Beautiful Gate of the temple. They were struck with astonishment —utterly stupefied at what had happened to him.

Luke 19:28-40
Palm Sunday Procession

Having spoken thus he went ahead with his ascent to Jerusalem. As he approached Bethphage and Bethany on the mount called Olivet, he sent two of the disciples with these instructions: "Go into the village straight ahead of you. Upon entering it you will find an ass tied there which no one has yet ridden. Untie it and bring it back. If anyone should ask you, 'Why are you untying the beast?' say, 'The Master has need of it.'"

They departed on their errand and found things just as he had said. As they untied the ass, its owner said to them, "Why are you doing that?" They explained that the Master needed it.

Then they led the animal to Jesus, and laying their cloaks on it, helped him mount. They spread their cloaks on the roadway as he moved along; and on his approach to the descent from Mount Olivet, the entire crowd of disciples began to rejoice and praise God loudly for the display of power they had seen, saying:

"Blessed be he who comes as king
in the name of the Lord!
Peace in heaven
and glory in the highest."

Some of the Pharisees in the crowd said to him. "Teacher, rebuke your disciples." He replied, "if they were to keep silence, I tell you the very stones would cry out."

DOMINUS FLEVIT

Taking the path down the Mount of Olives, the pilgrim comes to the entrance of the garden of the Chapel of Dominus Flevit (on the right). This commemorates the spot where Jesus wept over the city of Jerusalem.

Chapel of Dominus Flevit

Luke 19:41-44

Coming within sight of the city, he wept over it and said: "If only you had known the path to peace this day; but you have completely lost it from view! Days will come upon you when your enemies encircle you with a rampart, hem you in and press you hard from every side. They will wipe you out, you and your children within your walls, and leave not a stone on a stone within you, because you failed to recognize the time of your visitation."

Matthew 23:37-39

O Jerusalem, Jerusalem, murderess of prophets and stoner of those who were sent to you! How often have I yearned to gather your children as a mother hen gathers her young under her wings, but you refused me. Recall the saying, "You will find your temple deserted." I tell you, you will not see me from this time on until you declare, "Blessed is he who comes in the name of the Lord."

Revelation 21:1-4

Then I saw new heavens and a new earth. The former heavens and the former earth had passed away, and the sea was no longer. I also saw a new Jerusalem, the holy city, coming down out of heaven from God, beautiful as a bride prepared to meet her husband. I heard a loud voice from the throne cry out: "This is God's dwelling among men. He shall dwell with them and they shall be his people and he shall be their God who is always with them. He shall wipe every tear from their eyes, and there shall be no more death or mourning, crying out or pain, for the former world has passed away."

GARDEN OF GETHSEMANE

At the bottom of the Mount of Olives, below the White Russian Orthodox Church of St. Mary Magdalene with its

An Ancient Olive tree in the garden of Gethsemane.

golden onion domes is the Garden of Gethsemane — the
name means "olive press". The ancient trees in the Garden
of the Church of All Nations (so named because it was built
with donations from around the world) possibly go back to
the time of Jesus.

Inside the church, the soft glow of light coming through
the windows of violet-tinted alabaster creates an atmosphere of mourning and sorrow. In the center of the sanctuary a stone is venerated as the place where Jesus prayed the
night before he died.

Luke 22:39-53

Then he went out and made his way, as was his custom,
to the Mount of Olives; his disciples accompanied him.
On reaching the place he said to them. "Pray that you
may not be put to the test." He withdrew from them
about a stone's throw, then went down on his knees and
prayed in these words: "Father, if it is your will, take this
cup from me; yet not my will but yours be done." An
angel then appeared to him from heaven to strengthen
him. In his anguish he prayed with all the greater intensity, and his sweat became like drops of blood falling to
the ground. Then he rose from prayer and came to his
disciples, only to find them asleep, exhausted with grief.
He said to them "Why are you sleeping? Wake up, and
pray that you may not be subjected to the trial."

While he was still speaking a crowd came led by the
man named Judas, one of the Twelve. He approached
Jesus to embrace him. Jesus said to him, Judas, would
you betray the Son of Man with a kiss?" When the
companions of Jesus saw what was going to happen, they
said, "Lord, shall we use the sword?" One of them went
so far as to strike the slave of the high priest and cut off his
right ear. Jesus said in answer to their question.
"Enough! " Then he touched the ear and healed the man.

But to those who had come out against him — the chief
priests, the chiefs of the temple guard, and the ancients
—Jesus said, "Am I a criminal that you come out after me

armed with swords and clubs? When I was with you day after day in the temple you never raised a hand against me. But this is your hour — the triumph of darkness!"

Reflection
He came to fulfill the promise that he is Emmanuel, God with us. And we would not have him. We abandoned him and left him alone. Truly it was night. It was the dark night of indifference and rejection. Was ever a person so alone?

How sad when enemies abandon one, but when friends do it, where can one turn? Only to the Father! Abba (Daddy) shows the intimacy of Jesus' relationship which he shared with us. The Father of Light can still pierce the darkness and chaos. The agony of this garden will be exchanged for a garden with an empty tomb. "For those who love God, all things work together unto good" (Rom 8:28).

Prayer
Lord Jesus, "because you suffered and were tempted, you are able to help those who are tempted" (Heb 2:18). "In you we do not have a high priest who is unable to sympathize with our weaknesses, but one who is tempted in every way that we are" (Heb 4:15). We come to share in your sorrow and trial. Be with us in all of ours when the darkness clouds us and there is no light but you.

Grant this Saving Lord. Amen.

Hymns
Amazing Grace (page 171)
O Sacred Head (page 189)

THE CHURCH OF ST. STEPHEN
As one leaves the Garden of Gethsemane, straight ahead across the valley is the rarely opened Church of St. Stephen (Acts 7). To the right is the subterranean church, venerated

by the Orthodox as the location of the Tomb of Mary. To
the right of it, down the stairs, is a cave where Jesus is
thought to have come with his disciples.

BETHANY

The little village of Bethany with the adjoining village of
Bethphage was (and is) the area from which the Palm Sunday procession began. Bethany is on the road from Jerusalem to Jericho (or vice versa as Jesus traversed it.) The
beautiful little church commemorates three events in the life
of the Lord. 1) Here he stayed at the home of Martha and
Mary. 2) Here he raised Lazarus from the dead. 3) Here he
was anointed for his burial. A large monastery stood here in
Crusader times and, earlier still, a fifth-century Byzantine
church. Remains of both are still visible.

Up the hill the Orthodox church and the mosque testify to
the universal veneration of the spot. The so-called "Tomb of
Lazarus" is here.

The following biblical passages can be brought to life by
reading them facing the appropriate frescoes on the interior
wall of the church:

Luke 10:38-42

> On their journey Jesus entered a village where a
> woman named Martha welcomed him to her home. She
> had a sister named Mary, who seated herself at the Lord's
> feet and listened to his words. Martha, who was busy with
> all the details of hospitality, came to him and said, "Lord,
> are you not concerned that my sister has left me to do the
> household tasks all alone? Tell her to help me."
> The Lord in reply said to her: "Martha, Martha, you
> are anxious and upset about many things; one thing only

is required. Mary has chosen the better portion and she shall not be deprived of it."

John 11:1-44

There was a certain man named Lazarus who was sick. He was from Bethany, the village of Mary and her sister Martha. (This Mary whose brother Lazarus was sick was the one who anointed the Lord with perfume and dried his feet with her hair.) The sisters sent word to Jesus to inform him, "Lord, the one you love is sick." Upon hearing this, Jesus said:

"This sickness is not to end in death;
rather it is for God's glory,
that through it the Son of God may be glorified."

Jesus loved Martha and her sister and Lazarus very much. Yet, after hearing that Lazarus was sick, he stayed on where he was for two days more. Finally he said to his disciples, "Let us go back to Judea." "Rabbi," protested the disciples, "with the Jews only recently trying to stone you, you are going back up there again?" Jesus answered:

"Are there not twelve hours of daylight?
If a man goes walking by day he does not stumble
because he sees the world bathed in light.
But if he goes walking at night he will stumble
since there is no light in him."

After uttering these words, he added, "Our beloved Lazarus has fallen asleep, but I am going there to wake him." At this the disciples objected, "Lord, if he is asleep his life will be saved." Jesus had been speaking about his death, but they thought he meant sleep in the sense of slumber. Finally Jesus said plainly: "Lazarus is dead. For your sakes I am glad I was not there, that you may come to believe. In any event let us go to him." Then Thomas (the name means twin) said: "Let us go along, to die with him."

When Jesus arrived in Bethany, he found that Lazarus had already been in the tomb four days. The village was not far from Jerusalem — just under two miles — and many Jewish people had come out to console Martha and Mary over their brother. When Martha heard that Jesus was coming she went to meet him, while Mary sat at home. Martha said to Jesus, "Lord, if you had been here, my brother would never have died. Even now, I am sure that God will give you whatever you ask of him." "Your brother will rise again," Jesus assured her. "I know he will rise again," Martha replied, "in the resurrection on the last day." Jesus told her:

> "I am the resurrection and the life:
> whoever believes in me,
> though they should die, will come to life;
> and whoever is alive and believes in me
> will never die.

Do you believe this?" "Yes, Lord," she replied. "I have come to believe that you are the Messiah, the Son of God: he who is to come into the world."

When she had said this she went back and called her sister Mary. "The Teacher is here, asking for you," she whispered. As soon as Mary heard this, she got up and started out in his direction. (Actually Jesus had not yet come into the village but was still at the spot where Martha had met him.) The Jews who were in the house with Mary consoling her saw her get up quickly and go out, so they followed her, thinking she was going to the tomb to weep there. When Mary came to the place where Jesus was, seeing him, she fell at his feet and said to him, "Lord, if you had been here, my brother would never have died." When Jesus saw her weeping, and the Jews who had accompanied her also weeping he was troubled in spirit, moved by the deepest emotions. "Where have you laid him?" he asked. "Lord, come and see," they said. Jesus began to weep, which caused the Jews to remark, "See how much he loved him!" But some said, "He opened the eyes of that blind man. Why could he not have done something to stop this man from dying?" Once again troubled in spirit, Jesus approached the tomb.

It was a cave with a stone laid across it. "Take away the stone," Jesus directed. Martha, the dead man's sister, said to him, "Lord, it has been four days now; surely there will

be a stench!" Jesus replied, "Did I not assure you that if
you believed you would see the glory of God displayed?"
They then took away the stone and Jesus looked upward
and said:

> "Father, I thank you for having heard me.
> I know that you always hear me but I have said
>   this for the sake of the crowd,
> that they may believe that you sent me."

Having said this he called loudly, "Lazarus, come out!"
The dead man came out, bound hand and foot with linen
strips, his face wrapped in a cloth. "Untie him," Jesus told
them, "and let him go free."

Matthew 26:6-13

While Jesus was in Bethany at the house of Simon the
leper, a woman carrying a jar of costly perfume came up
to him at table and began to pour it on his head. When the
disciples saw this they grew indignant, protesting: "What
is the point of such extravagance? This could have been
sold for a good price and the money given to the poor."
Jesus became aware of this and said to them: "Why do
you criticize the woman? It is a good deed she has done
for me. The poor you will always have with you but you
will not always have me. By pouring this perfume on my
body, she has contributed toward my burial preparation.
I assure you, wherever the good news is proclaimed
throughout the world, what she did will be spoken of as
her memorial."

Reflection

The home of Martha and Mary is the scene of one of the
greatest breakthroughs in the history of religion. Here Jesus
revealed the revolutionary idea that women could be disciples. This was unheard of among the rabbis. He invites
Mary into that new and intimate relationship to which he
has already called the twelve. "In Christ Jesus, there is
neither slave nor free, Jew nor Gentile, male or female. We
are all one in Christ Jesus." Martha is not wrong, she is just
so preoccupied that she is missing this marvelous opportun-

ity. She is so busy that she misses the invitation of the Lord. She may be the first, but she is certainly not the last who misses the Lord's invitation.

Prayer
With Mary at the Master's feet, let us make known our needs to him.
- *For Women everywhere that they may achieve their rightful place in society*
   Let us pray to the Lord. Lord hear our prayer.
- *For families, that all who visit them may find Jesus in their midst...*
- *For a strengthening of family life and values___*
- *For all who have died or will die this day, that the Lord who raised Lazarus, will give them the light and peace of his kingdom...*

God, Our Father, your Son loved to visit this home. Here he found the companionship and joy of a loving family. Bless our homes. Strengthen our families. Send your Son to abide with us. This we ask through Christ, Our Lord. Amen.

Hymn
Whatsoever You Do   (page 201)

THE INN OF THE GOOD SAMARITAN

Halfway between Jerusalem and Jericho are the remains of an old caravanserei which housed travellers and protected their animals overnight. They were placed strategically so that they stood a day's journey apart. Since Jesus' story is a parable it is a bit unrealistic to be looking for the address of the Good Samaritan Hospital. Nevertheless, the location can bring the story to life.

Luke 10:25-37

On one occasion a lawyer stood up to pose him this problem: "Teacher, what must I do to inherit everlasting life?" Jesus answered him: "What is written in the law? How do you read it?" He replied:

"You shall love the Lord your God
with all your heart,
with all your soul,
with all your strength,
and with all your mind;
and your neighbor as yourself."

Jesus said, "You have answered correctly. Do this and you shall live." But because he wished to justify himself he said to Jesus, "And who is my neighbor?" Jesus replied: "There was a man going down from Jerusalem to Jericho who fell prey to robbers. They stripped him, beat him and then went off leaving him half-dead. A priest happened to be going down the same road; he saw him but continued on. Likewise there was a Levite who came the same way; he saw him but continued on. But a Samaritan who was journeying along came on him and was moved to pity at the sight. He approached him and dressed his wounds, pouring on oil and wine. He then hoisted him on his own beast and brought him to an inn, where he cared for him. The next day he took out two silver pieces and gave them to the innkeeper with the request: 'Look after him, and if there is any further expense I will repay you on my way back.'

"Which of these three, in your opinion, was neighbor to the man who fell in with the robbers?" The answer came, "The one who treated him with compassion." Jesus said to him, "Then go and do the same."

Hymn

Where Charity and Love Prevail (page 202)

QUMRAN

Although not a Biblical site, Qumran, like Masada about thirty miles to the south, is well worth a visit. Here in the Judean Desert lived a community of Essenes, a strict sect of

Wadi Qumran and Cave 4, where some of the most important scrolls were discovered.

Judaism, who were contemporaries of Jesus and the Baptist. They lived in the wilderness awaiting God's judgment on the world. Suspected by the Romans of being collaborators in insurrection, their settlement was destroyed in 68 A.D. The community hid their library in nearby caves and were dispersed. Some may have become Christian (2 Cor 6:14-7:1 seems to have been inserted by a hand from Qumran). The Dead Sea Scrolls were discovered by a nomad boy chasing a stray goat in 1947. They have had a profound affect on modern Biblical studies.

JERICHO

After the barrenness of the Desert of Judea, and the funereal waters of the Dead Sea, the lowest spot on the face of the earth, one appreciates more than ever what an oasis is. The vendors of fresh fruit and freshly squeezed juices heighten the impression of a place of refreshment.

This is the site of the oldest city on earth. On his last journey Jesus passed through here on his way to Jerusalem. Local Arabs (Moslem and Christian) point out a picturesque sycamore tree beneath which the story of Zachaeus can be read, preferably in parts.

Luke 19:1-10

Narrator: Entering Jericho, he passed through the city. There was a man there named Zachaeus, the chief tax collector and a wealthy man. He was trying to see what Jesus was like, but being small of stature was unable to do so because of the crowd. He first ran on in front, then climbed a sycamore tree which was on Jesus' route, in order to see him. When Jesus came to the spot, he looked up.

Jesus: Zachaeus, hurry down. I mean to stay at your house today.

Narrator: He quickly jumped down and welcomed him with delight. When this was observed, everyone began murmuring, "He has gone to a sinner's house as a guest." Zachaeus stood his ground.

Zachaeus: Lord, I give half my belongings to the poor. If I have defrauded anyone in the least, I pay them back fourfold."

Jesus: Today, salvation has come to this house, for this is what it means to be a son of Abraham. The Son of Man has come to search out and save that which was lost.

IN AND AROUND JERICHO

The little church of the Good Shepherd, surrounded by a fine school run by the Franciscan sisters, and a playground where youngsters frolic like lambs, is a good place to reflect on Jesus as the Good Shepherd.

John 10:11-18

"I am the good shepherd;
the good shepherd lays down his life for the sheep.
The hired hand — who is no shepherd
nor owner of the sheep —
catches sight of the wolf coming
and runs away, leaving the sheep
to be snatched and scattered by the wolf.
That is because he works for pay;
he has no concern for the sheep.
I am the good shepherd.
I know my sheep
and my sheep know me
in the same way that the Father knows me
and I know the Father;
for these sheep I will give my life.
I have other sheep
that do not belong to this fold.
I must lead them too,
and they shall hear my voice.
There shall be one flock then, one shepherd.
The Father loves me for this:
That I lay down my life to take it up again.
No one takes it from me; I lay it down freely.
I have power to lay it down,
and I have power to take it up again.
This command I received from my Father."

MOUNT OF TEMPTATION

High above Jericho is Jebel Quruntul (Mount of the Quarantine or forty days). Tradition, attested to by the ancient Greek Monastery that clings to the side of the mountain, holds that this is the mountain upon which Jesus was tempted.

The Mount of Temptation and the ancient Greek Monastery

Matthew 4:1-4 and 8-11

Then Jesus was led into the desert by the Spirit to be tempted by the devil. He fasted forty days and forty nights, and afterward was hungry. The tempter approached and said to him, "If you are the Son of God, command these stones to turn into bread." Jesus replied, "Scripture has it:

'Not on bread alone is man to live
but on every utterance that comes from the
mouth of God.'"

The devil then took him up a very high mountain and
displayed before him all the kingdoms of the world in
their magnificence, promising, "All these will I bestow on
you if you prostrate yourself in homage before me." At
this Jesus said to him, "Away with you, Satan! Scripture
has it:

'You shall do homage to the Lord your God;
him alone shall you adore."

At that the devil left him, and angels came and waited
on him.

ANCIENT JERICHO (Tell es Sultan)

The great mound really calls for a guide well versed in
archaeology. Even driving by, however, one can see the
trenches cut in the sides to reveal the habitation levels of
centuries. Since hardly anything was found indicating occu-
pation at the time of Joshua's invasion, scholars dispute
whether or not this is the site actually referred to in Jos. 6.

MOUNT NEBO

What is not disputed, however, is that Mount Nebo to the
East, across the Jordan, is the spot from which Moses
viewed the promised land before his death. It was from there
that he sent the Israelites to receive God's gift which he had
promised through Abraham: "Go forth from the land of
your kinsfolk and from your father's house to a land that I
will show you" (Gen 12:1).

Deuteronomy 34

"Then Moses went up from the plains of Moab to Mt.
Nebo ... which faces Jericho, and the Lord showed him
all the land ... The Lord then said to him, 'This is the
land which I swore to Abraham, Issac and Jacob, that I
would give to their descendants. I have let you feast your
eyes on it, but you shall not cross over.' So there ...
Moses died ... Since then, no prophet has arisen in Israel
like Moses, whom the Lord knew face to face."

PART III

HOLY PLACES
WEST OF JERUSALEM

HOLY PLACES
WEST OF JERUSALEM

EMMAUS

About seven miles from Jerusalem, toward the coast, is the small town of Qubeiba or Emmaus. One tradition holds that this is the spot where Jesus' two disciples recognized him in the breaking of the Bread on Easter Sunday. The present church is built on the ruins of the 900-year-old Crusader church, clearly visible inside. On the facade is a lovely glazed terra-cotta depiction of the Lucan scene. This quiet place, with its splendid view of the hill country toward the Mediterranean, is an oasis of prayerful peace after the turmoil of Jerusalem.

Luke 24:13-35

Two of them that same day were making their way to a village named Emmaus, seven miles distant from Jerusalem, discussing as they went all that had happened. In the course of their lively exchange, Jesus approached and began to walk along with them. However, they were restrained from recognizing him. He said to them, "What are you discussing as you go your way?" They halted, in distress, and one of them, Cleopas by name, asked him,

"Are you the only resident of Jerusalem who does not know the things that went on there these past few days?" He said to them, "What things?" They said: "All those that had to do with Jesus of Nazareth, a prophet powerful in word and deed in the eyes of God and all the people, how our chief priests and leaders delivered him up to be condemned to death, and crucified him. We were hoping that he was the one who would set Israel free. Besides all this, today, the third day since these things happened, some women of our group have just brought us some astonishing news. They were at the tomb before dawn and failed to find his body, but returned with the tale that they had seen a vision of angels who declared he was alive. Some of our number went to the tomb and found it to be just as the women said, but him they did not see."

Then he said to them, "What little sense you have! How slow you are to believe all that the prophets have announced! Did not the Messiah have to undergo all this so as to enter into his Glory?" Beginning then with Moses and all the prophets, he interpreted for them every passage of Scripture which referred to him. By now they were near the village to which they were going, and he acted as if he were going farther. But they pressed him: "Stay with us. It is nearly evening — the day is practically over." So he went in to stay with them.

When he had seated himself with them to eat, he took bread, pronounced the blessing, then broke the bread and began to distribute it to them. With that their eyes were opened and they recognized him; whereupon he vanished from their sight. They said to one another, "Were not our hearts burning inside us as he talked to us on the road and explained the Scriptures to us?" They got up immediately and returned to Jerusalem, where they found the Eleven and the rest of the company assembled. They were greeted with, "The Lord has been raised! It is true! He has appeared to Simon." Then they recounted what had happened on the road and how they had come to know him in the breaking of bread.

Reflection

The great danger of a pilgrimage like this is that it may lead some to spend a lot of time wishing they could be back there listening and talking to Jesus.

Luke, who recounts this story, is like ourselves. He had never seen Jesus, but got his material from those who had. He recalls this event to prevent the daydreaming that may hinder us from recognizing a presence of Jesus that is available to us.

We are those two disciples, living in the past, reminiscing over the "good old days." They grieve that Jesus is not with them any more. He appears, almost playing a game with them, trying to get them to stop taking themselves so seriously.

He shows them how he is still with them. They can find him in the Scriptures. He is always present in the Word. If, instead of dreaming about what might have been, they had gone to God's Word, they would have found him. Even Jesus tells them their problem was not his absence from them, but that they were foolish and slow of heart. When he led them through the Scriptures which revealed him, he caused their hearts to burn within them. He still does. He still can be found there.

Later, they recognized him in the breaking of the bread. It is the same today. We need not yearn for a presence that is past or faraway. We can hear him in the Word and find him in the breaking of the Bread each time we gather in his Name.

Prayer

Lord Jesus, walk with us on our way. Let your words burn within us so that our hearts may never grow cold. Awaken us to the reality of your presence in your life-giving Word, and in the breaking of the bread.

This we ask, O Risen Lord! Amen.

Hymns
Let Us Break Bread Together (page 186)
Where Charity and Love Prevail   (page 202)

AIN KAREM

THE CHURCH OF THE NATIVITY
OF JOHN THE BAPTIST

In the foothills of Judea is the quiet little town associated with the birth of John the Baptist and the Visitation of Mary to her cousin, Elizabeth.

The Church of the Nativity of John the Baptist has long been in the care of the Spanish Franciscans. The splendid blue-glazed tiles and the masterpieces by such great artists as Murillo and Ribalta were the gifts of the people of Spain over the centuries. To the left of the sanctuary is the staircase to the cave which was thought to be part of the home of Zachary and Elizabeth.

Luke 1:57-79

When Elizabeth's time for delivery arrived, she gave birth to a son. Her neighbors and relatives, upon hearing that the Lord had extended his mercy to her, rejoiced with her. When they assembled for the circumcision of the child on the eighth day, they intended to name him after his father Zechariah. At this his mother intervened, saying, "No, he is to be called John."

They pointed out to her, "None of your relatives has this name." Then, using signs, they asked the father what he wished him to be called. He signaled for a writing tablet and wrote the words, "His name is John." This astonished them all. At that moment his mouth was opened and his tongue loosed, and he began to speak in praise of God.

Steeple of Church of St. John the Baptist.

Fear descended on all in the neighborhood; through-out the hill country of Judea these happenings began to be recounted to the last detail. All who heard stored these things up in their hearts, saying, "What will this child be?" and, "Was not the hand of the Lord upon him?"

Zechariah's Canticle. Then Zechariah, his father, filled with the Holy Spirit, uttered this prophecy:

> Blessed be the Lord the God of Israel,
> because he has visited and ransomed his people.
> He has raised a horn of saving strength for us
> in the house of David his servant,
> as he promised through the mouths of his holy
> ones,
> the prophets of ancient times,
> salvation from our enemies
> and from the hands of all our foes.
> He has dealt mercifully with our fathers
> and remembered the holy covenant he made,
> the oath he swore to Abraham our father, he

would grant us
that, rid of fear and delivered from the enemy,
we should serve him devoutly and through all
    our days
be holy in his sight.
And you, O child, shall be called
prophet of the Most High;
for you shall go before the Lord
to prepare straight paths for him,
giving his people a knowledge of salvation
in freedom from their sins.
All this is the work of the kindness of our God:
he, the Dayspring, shall visit us in his mercy,
to shine on those who sit in darkness
and in the shadow of death,
    to guide our feet into the way of peace."
    The child grew up and matured in spirit. He lived in the
desert until the day when he made his public appearance
in Israel.

THE CHURCH OF THE VISITATION

Leaving the Church of St. John and crossing the road,
one finds the roofed-over spring (*ain, ein,* or *en*) after which
the village gets its name. The hill to the right requires good
legs and stamina — the climb is well worth the effort. At the
top is the Church of the Visitation — built above an earlier
Crusader church. The gates open on to a peaceful courtyard
where the Magnificat is inscribed on ceramic plaques in a
multitude of languages.

The lower church is meant to mark the home of Elizabeth.
A cave to the right contains an ancient cistern. In a niche
stands a boulder which according to legend, opened to
swallow the infant Baptist, and saved him from Herod's
soldiers during the massacre of the Innocents!

The modern church, reached by an outside staircase, is a
poem in stone and a celebration of color and light. Like
Mary's song of praise, it lifts one up to the Lord. The fresco

over the sanctuary recalls the different religious orders named after Mary and the major shrines throughout the world dedicated to her. Those on the side wall recall moments of church history concerning the Mother of God.

Luke 1:39-56

Thereupon Mary set out, proceeding in haste into the hill country to a town of Judah, where she entered Zechariah's house and greeted Elizabeth. When Elizabeth heard Mary's greeting, the baby leapt in her womb. Elizabeth was filled with the Holy Spirit and cried out in a loud voice: "Blest are you among women and blest is the fruit of your womb. But who am I that the mother of my Lord should come to me? The moment your greeting sounded in my ears, the baby leapt in my womb for joy. Blest is she who trusted the Lord's words to her would be fulfilled."

Mary's Canticle. Then Mary said:

"My being proclaims the greatness of the Lord,
my spirit finds joy in God my savior,
for he has looked upon his servant in her lowliness;
all ages to come shall call me blessed.
God who is mighty has done great things for me,
holy is his name;
his mercy is from age to age
on those who fear him.
He has shown might with his arm;
he has confused the proud in their inmost thoughts.
He has deposed the mighty from their thrones
and raised the lowly to high places.
The hungry he has given every good thing,
while the rich he has sent empty away.
He has upheld Israel his servant,
ever mindful of his mercy;
even as he promised our fathers,
promised Abraham and his descendants forever."

Mary remained with Elizabeth about three months and then returned home.

Reflection

The mystery of the Mother of God is the mystery of the Church and of every Christian. It is the wonder of God's grace at work in us. He who is mighty has done great things indeed. Mary is a living witness to that. Like her, each of us is called to go in haste to our neighbor. We are called to be living Magnificats who praise and glorify the Lord.

Prayer

Father, you sent Mary, the New Ark of the Covenant, on the first Christian pilgrimage in your Holy Land. She bore the Divine Presence in your Son. At that Presence, the infant Baptist jumped for joy. Fill our hearts with rejoicing. Help us never to forget the mighty things that you have done for us. We praise and magnify your name through Jesus, the Lord, Amen.

Hymn

Cf. Magnificat to the tune of Amazing Grace (page 187)

HADASSAH HOSPITAL

Above the village of Ain Karem is the excellent Hadassah hospital built by the American Jewish Women's Organization. Its synagogue contains Chagal's stained glass windows of the twelve tribes of Israel, one of the masterpieces of modern art (cf. The Testament of Jacob to his twelve sons, Gen 49).

PART IV

HOLY PLACES
SOUTH OF JERUSALEM

HOLY PLACES
SOUTH OF JERUSALEM

BETHLEHEM

TOMB OF RACHEL

The 15-minute ride to Bethlehem passes by Tantur, the ecumenical-theological center established by Pope Paul VI and run by Notre Dame University. At the approach to the "Little Town" is the Tomb of Rachel.

Matthew 2:16-18

Once Herod realized that he had been deceived by the astrologers, he became furious. He ordered the massacre of all the boys two years old and under in Bethlehem and its environs, making his calculations on the basis of the date he had learned from the astrologers. What was said through Jeremiah the prophet was then fulfilled:

"A cry was heard at Ramah,
sobbing and loud lamentation:
Rachel bewailing her children;
no comfort for her,
since they are no more."

THE CHURCH OF THE NATIVITY

Manger Square, with its merchants of carved olive wood creches and mother-of-pearl jewelry, stands in front of one of the most ancient churches of Christendom. It is in the charge of the Greek Orthodox. Centuries ago the spacious door was reduced to the small one of today so that one must bow low to enter the spot where God humbled himself to become man. It was done for a less spiritual reason: to prevent looting invaders from riding in on horse-back. The interior of the church still contains elements from the fourth-century Church of St. Helena, such as the mosaic floor beneath the wooden doors of the present level. To the right of the Orthodox sanctuary a staircase descends to the cave of the Nativity. The silver star beneath the Greek altar proclaims in Latin that "Here the Word was made Flesh." To the side are the Latin altars of the Manger and the Adoration by the Magi.

Luke 2:1-7

In those days Caesar Augustus published a decree ordering a census of the whole world. This first census took place while Quirinius was governor of Syria. Everyone went to register, each to his own town. And so Joseph went from the town of Nazareth in Galilee to Judea, to David's town of Bethlehem — because he was of the house and lineage of David — to register with Mary, his espoused wife, who was with child.

While they were there the days of her confinement were completed. She gave birth to her first-born son and wrapped him swaddling clothes and laid him in a manger, because there was no room for them in the place where travelers lodged.

John 1:18

In the beginning was the Word; the Word was in God's presence, and the Word was God. He was present to god in the beginning. Through him all things came into being, and apart from him nothing came to be. Whatever came to be in him, found life, life for the light of men. The light

Manger Square and the courtyard of the Church of the Nativity

shines on in darkness, a darkness that did not overcome it.

He was in the world, and through him the world was made, yet the world did not know who he was. To his own, he came, yet his own did not accept him. Any who did accept him he empowered to become children of God.

These are they who believe in his name — who were begotten not by blood, nor by carnal desire, nor by man's willing it, but by God.

The Word became flesh
and made his dwelling among us,

and we have seen his glory:
The glory of an only Son coming from the Father,
filled with enduring love.
Of his fullness
we have all had a share—
love following upon love.

For while the law was given through Moses, this enduring
love came through Jesus Christ. No one has ever seen
God. It is God the only Son, ever at the Father's side, who
has revealed him.

Matthew 2:1-11

After Jesus' birth in Bethlehem of Judea during the reign
of King Herod, astrologers from the east arrived one day
in Jerusalem inquiring "Where is the newborn king of the
Jews? We observed his star at its rising and have come to
pay him homage." At this news King Herod became
greatly disturbed, and with him all Jerusalem. Summon-
ing all of the chief priests and scribes of the people, he
inquired of them where the Messiah was to be born. "In
Bethlehem of Judea," they informed him. "Here is what
the prophet has written:

'And you, Bethlehem, land of Judah,
are by no means least among the princes of
    Judah,
since from you shall come a ruler
who is to shepherd my people Israel.'"

Herod called the astrologers aside and found out from
them the exact time of the star's appearance. Then he sent
them to Bethlehem, after having instructed them: "Go
and get detailed information about the child. When you
have found him, report it to me so that I may go and offer
him homage too."

After their audience with the king, they set out. The
star which they had observed at its rising went ahead of
them until it came to a standstill over the place where the
child was. They were overjoyed at seeing the star, and on
entering the house, found the child with Mary his
Mother. They prostrated themselves and did him hom-

age. Then they opened their coffers and presented him with gifts of gold, frankincense, and myrrh.

Reflection

Kneel before the place where the "Word was made flesh, and dwelt among us." Know that he loved us so much that "he became like us in everything!" There is no part of our humanity that he did not embrace. He loved and laughed. He cried and cringed. He sweated and sighed. Surely Augustine is right when he says that the only line of the New Testament that is so unique that it can be found nowhere else is "The Word was made flesh and dwelt among us." He shared our humanity that we might share his divinity, for: "to as many as received him, he gave the power to become the children of God."

Prayer

Father, we kneel before him who is the image of the invisible God, the firstborn of all creation. (Col 1) Here, your eternal plan is fulfilled. We fall on our knees before him for whom you made the universe. He is the world's center of gravity and the very heartbeat of creation. Thank you for the overflowing love which burst forth and is found in the arms of Mary. With the fire of that love, melt the iciness of our hearts, that we may proclaim "Jesus is Lord." Amen.

Hymns

Silent Night   (page 204)
O Come All Ye Faithful   (page 205)
We Three Kings   (page 198)
Children Sing With Voices Gay   (page 176)

CHURCH OF ST. CATHERINE

Ascending the stairs to the left brings us to the area where the Armenian Orthodox worship, and to the entrance to the Church of St. Catherine. Since history has deprived the Latin Rite Catholics of all but a tiny area of the basilica, they have built a church which for some obscure reason is dedicated to the Patroness of Philosophers, St. Catherine of Alexandria. The Christmas Eve Mass that is televised throughout the world is broadcast from here.

At the rear of the church the staircase descends to other caves dedicated to the memory of the Holy Innocents, and St. Joseph, and to St. Jerome, who lived in his cave, studying and translating the Bible into Latin (known as the Vulgate). His statue is on a pedestal in the cloister in front of the church.

SHEPHERD'S FIELD

To find the peace so necessary for prayer go to Shepherd's Field outside the city. Here, where shepherds traditionally tended their sheep, is a cave where liturgy may be celebrated after arrangement. There is also a lovely chapel donated by Canadian Catholics. The friar at the spot will usually give permission to ring the bells while you sing the "Gloria," or "Angels We Have Heard on High."

Luke 2:8-18

There were shepherds in that locality, living in the fields and keeping night watch by turns over their flocks. The angel of the Lord appeared to them as the glory of the Lord shone around them, and they were very much afraid. The angel said to them: "You have nothing to fear! I come to proclaim good news to you — tidings of great joy to be shared by the whole people. This day in David's city a savior has been born to you, the Messiah and Lord. Let this be a sign to you: in a manger you will find an infant wrapped in swaddling clothes." Suddenly, there was with the angel a multitude of the heavenly host, praising God and saying,

"Glory to God in high heaven,

peace on earth to those on whom his favor rests."

When the angels had returned to heaven, the shepherds said to one another: "Let us go over to Bethlehem and see this event which the Lord has made known to us." They went in haste and found Mary and Joseph and the baby lying in the manger; once they saw, they understood what had been told them concerning this child. All who heard of it were astonished at the report given them by the shepherds.

Reflection

"The Glory of God is man fully alive" (St. Irenaeus). To be fully alive! This was no longer a dream, for the Son of God had come "That they may have life and have it abundantly" (Jn 10:10). The news did not come to the priests. They were too busy with "religion." It did not come to King Herod, busy trying to run the world. It came to the shepherds, poorest of the poor, migrant workers and outcasts of society.

They were looked down upon, but in their night vigils they had been looking up at the sky, the moon and the stars. They had watched the miracle of lambs being born. They had never lost their sense of wonder at creation, so they were close to their Creator. Suddenly they were invited to the New Creation in Christ the Lord.

They were told that the age of Peace had dawned. In aramaic, the language of Jesus, Peace is "Shalom." It means to be complete, to be whole, to live up to your potential, to be everything you are capable of becoming, to be fully alive to the Glory of God.

The sophisticated upper classes and clerical ranks in Jerusalem, only a few miles away, looked down on the shepherds as being deprived, lacking the social graces so necessary for life in "proper" society. But the shepherds had a secret, so marvelous that the angels could not just speak it, they had to sing it out. It is the same secret, the same mystery now revealed to us. Come to Jesus, your savior and Lord. Here is life to the full. Live in him, and give glory to God.

Prayer
Almighty God and Father of our Lord Jesus Christ, the light has come into the darkness and the darkness could not overpower it. It is the fullness of time. It is the apex of history and only a few shepherds were open enough to be told of it. We join our faith with theirs, and our voices with the angels: "Glory to God in the highest." Grant to us that peace which the angels announced. We ask this in the name of Jesus, the Lord. Amen.

Hymn
Angels We Have Heard on High   (page 206)

HEBRON

The combination mosque-synagogue testifies to the fact that Abraham, whom Christians revere as our father in faith, is jointly honored by Arab and Jew as their common ancestor. The building, from Herod's time, is built over the cave of Machpelah which Abraham bought to serve as a tomb. There, the Patriarchs and some of their wives were interred.

Genesis 25:7-11
> The whole span of Abraham's life was one hundred and seventy-five years. Then he breathed his last, dying at

a ripe old age, grown old after a full life; and he was taken to his kinsmen. His sons Isaac and Ishmael buried him in the cave of Machpelah, in the field of Ephron, son of Zohar the Hittite, which faces Mamre, the field that Abraham bought from the Hittites; there he was buried next to his wife Sarah. After the death of Abraham, God blessed his son Isaac.

Hymn
Faith of Our Fathers (page 181)

PART V

HOLY PLACES
NORTH OF JERUSALEM

HOLY PLACES
NORTH OF JERUSALEM

SAMARIA

North of Jerusalem are several cities, such as Bethel and Shechem, associated with the Patriarchs and the early history of Israel. In the ninth century B.C. when the tribes split into the two nations of Israel and Juda, the northern kingdom created a rival capital at Samaria. Eventually, on Mount Gerizim a temple was built to compete with the one in Jerusalem. Sacrifice is still carried out on the spot at Passover time by the Samaritan High Priest. The city was destroyed by the Assyrians in 721 B.C. and the leaders deported into exile (hence, the lost ten tribes of Israel). The remnant populace intermarried with foreigners who were brought in to occupy the land. The Samaritans, because of their mixed blood and schismatic cult, were avoided by the Jews. Jacob's well in the lower part of the Greek church bears witness to the ancient Biblical relevance of the place now called Nablus.

John 4:4-24

> He had to pass through Samaria and his journey brought him to a Samaritan town named Shechem near the plot of land which Jacob had given to his son Joseph.

This was the site of Jacob's well. Jesus, tired from his journey, sat down at the well.

The hour was about noon. When a Samaritan woman came to draw water, Jesus said to her, "Give me a drink." (His disciples had gone off to the town to buy provisions.) The Samaritan woman said to him, "You are a Jew. How can you ask me, a Samaritan and a woman, for a drink?" (Recall that Jews have nothing to do with Samaritans.) Jesus replied:

> "If only you recognized God's gift, and who it is
> that is asking you for a drink,
> you would have asked him instead, and he would
> have given you living water."

"Sir," she challenged him, "you do not have a bucket and this well is deep. Where do you expect to get this flowing water? Surely you do not pretend to be greater than our ancestor Jacob, who gave us this well and drank from it with his sons and his flocks?" Jesus replied:

> "Everyone who drinks this water
> will be thirsty again.
> But whoever drinks the water I give him
> will never be thirsty;
> no, the water I give
> shall become a fountain within him,
> leaping up to provide eternal life."

The woman said to him, "Give me this water sir, so that I shall not grow thirsty, and have to keep coming here to draw water."

He said to her, "Go, call your husband, and then come back here." "I have no husband," replied the woman. "You are right in saying you have no husband!" Jesus exclaimed. "The fact is, you have had five, and the man you are living with now is not your husband. What you said is true."

"Sir," answered the woman. "I can see you are a prophet. Our ancestors worshipped on this mountain, but you people claim that Jerusalem is the place where one ought to worship God." Jesus told her:

> "Believe me, woman, an hour is coming

when you will worship the Father
neither on this mountain nor in Jerusalem.
You people worship what you do not understand,
while we understand what we worship;
after all, salvation is from the Jews.
Yet an hour is coming, and is already here,
when authentic worshippers
will worship the Father in Spirit and truth.
Indeed, it is just such worshippers the Father seeks.
God is Spirit, and those who worship him
must worship in Spirit and truth."
The woman said to him: "I know there is a Messiah coming. (This term means Anointed.) When he comes, he will tell us everything. Jesus replied, "I who speak to you am he."

Acts 8:4-8

Now those who were scattered went about preaching the word. Philip went down to a city of Samaria, and proclaimed to them the Christ. And the multitudes with one accord gave heed to what was said by Philip, when they heard him and saw the signs which he did. For unclean spirits came out of many who were possessed, crying with a loud voice; and many who were paralyzed or lame were healed. So there was much joy in that city. (R.S.V.)

MEGIDDO

Between Southern Galilee and Northern Samaria is the lush and fertile plain of Megiddo. Known also as the Valley of Jezreel, it was the scene of horrible bloodshed and carnage in ancient wars. To show his dissatisfaction with the constant strife of his people, Hosea was told at the birth of his son:

"Give him the name Jezreel;
for in a little while
I will punish the house of Jehu [King of Israel]

for the bloodshed at Jezreel
and bring to an end the kingdom
of the house of Israel. (Hos 1:3)

Legend took up the memory and saw this area as the scene
of the final battle of history (Armageddon = Mountain of
Megiddo; cf. Rev 16:16). The excavations at Megiddo have
uncovered a fortified city built by Solomon (1 Kgs 9:15).

NAZARETH

Not thought worthy of mention in the entire Old Testament, Nazareth was considered to be provincial and back-
ward. "Philip sought out Nathaniel and told him ... 'We
have found the one Moses spoke of in the law and the
prophets, too — Jesus, son of Joseph from Nazareth.'
Nathaniel's response was "Can anything good come from
Nazareth?" and Philip replied, "Come and see for yourself!"
(Jn 1:45-46). We come to see for ourselves.

BASILICA OF THE ANNUNCIATION

Dominating the town of Nazareth today is the recently
finished Basilica of the Annunciation. To visit it is to enter
the most beautiful church in the Holy Land. In the crypt can
be seen the cave which was part of the house of Mary, where
the mystery of the Incarnation took place. Recent archaeological work has found graffiti indicating very early Christian veneration of the spot. (During the day the gates of the
cave are locked, but early in the morning, if no services are
going on, pilgrims are permitted to enter and pray.)

Outside the cave sanctuary to the left, a dedication plaque
was uncovered declaring that a basilica was built in the early
400's by a Deacon Conon of Jerusalem. Though the floor of
this Byzantine church is lower than the present crypt, the
outline of its walls and sanctuary are clearly visible in the
modern church. By the year 1100 this Byzantine church was
covered by the immense Crusader Basilica whose walls can

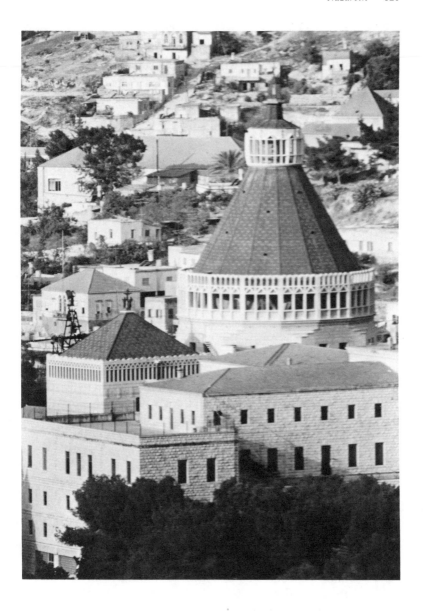

Basilica of the Annunciation.

be seen behind the cave sanctuary. The hewn stones are in contrast to the poured concrete of the modern basilica which is almost the exact size of the Crusader church.

That church stood only about 150 years. The Franciscans bought the property in 1620. One hundred and twenty years later, they were permitted to put up a modest sanctuary on the previous ruins. Some elements of that, such as pillars and altar, are preserved in and around the cave. The upper floor serves as the parish church of the Catholic Arab community of Nazareth. The mosaic in the sanctuary depicts the Constitution on the Church of Vatican Council II. (When services are in progress for the parish the entire basilica is closed to all visitors.)

Luke 1:26-38

In the sixth month, the angel Gabriel was sent from God to a town of Galilee named Nazareth, to a virgin betrothed to a man named Joseph, of the house of David. The virgin's name was Mary. Upon arriving the angel said to her: "Rejoice, O highly favored daughter! The Lord is with you. Blessed are you among women." She was deeply troubled by his words, and wondered what his greeting meant. The angel went on to say to her: "Do not fear, Mary. You have found favor with God. You shall conceive and bear a son and give him the name Jesus. Great will be his dignity and he will be called Son of the Most High. The Lord God will give him the throne of David his father. He will rule over the house of Jacob forever and his reign will be without end."

Mary said to the angel, "How can this be since I do not know man?" The angel answered her: "The Holy Spirit will come upon you and the power of the Most High will overshadow you; hence, the holy offspring to be born will be called Son of God. Know that Elizabeth your kinswoman has conceived a son in her old age; she who was thought to be sterile is now in her sixth month, for nothing is impossible with God."

Mary said: "I am the servant of the Lord. Let it be done to me as you say." With that the angel left her.

Reflection

Three times a day, throughout the world, many Christians recite the "Angelus": "The angel of the Lord declared unto Mary. And she conceived by the Holy Spirit. The Word was made flesh, and dwelt among us." Only on this sacred spot is another word added to that prayer: *Here* the Word was made flesh. Here the young maiden, because she had already conceived the word in her heart, was able to say "Yes, be it done unto me according to your word," and conceive the Word in her womb.

A pilgrimage to this spot is like walking through history, for the genius of the architect has incorporated every previous church through the centuries into it. We can go all the way back to the "Here the Word was made flesh" of the earliest Christians. Fleeing from the destruction of Jerusalem with its Temple, they came to the spot where the New Temple of God came among us. They came, as did succeeding generations, as witnesses to the fact that "In him was life, and the life was the light of men. The Light shines in the darkness, and the darkness has not overcome it" (Jn 1:4-5).

The lingering question, as we honor the Lord here, is why was he accepted by so few? Was he so strange that they could not recognize him? Was he so different that he was beyond their expectations? No. The problem was that he was too much like themselves. So many had already decided how God should act, how He should come among them. They had forgotten that the Lord had spoken through Isaiah: "For my thoughts are not your thoughts, neither are your ways my ways" (Is 55:8).

Nazareth. The Annunciation. The Incarnation. Here are our warnings to keep ourselves open to the Lord, wherever and however he may manifest himself. He is the God of surprises who comes in amazing ways. Be surprised, be amazed, be open. He is Emmanuel — God with us. But in ways we did not expect.

Prayer

Father, we venerate the place where you proved that you are not a God who is distant and uncaring. We venerate the mystery of your presence and closeness. Jesus is Emmanuel, God with us.

Show us how, like Mary, we may have hearts open to your Word. You still want to send your Son into the world. Help us say again "Be it done unto us according to your word." This we ask through Jesus, the Word made Flesh. Amen.

Hymns

O Come O Come Emmanuel (page 188)
Sing of Mary (page 172)

ST. JOSEPH'S CHURCH

Exiting through the side door of the upper church we come to the Baptistry. Up the steps, keeping the Friary and Terra Sancta College to the right, we come to the Church of St. Joseph. In the crypt are cisterns and storage areas showing that this was the business and commercial area of Nazareth.

Matthew 1:18-25

> Now this is how the birth of Jesus Christ came about. When his mother Mary was engaged to Joseph, but before they lived together, she was found with child through the power of the Holy Spirit. Joseph her husband, an upright man unwilling to expose her to the law, decided to divorce her quietly. Such was his intention when suddenly the angel of the Lord appeared in a dream and said to him: "Joseph," son of David, have no fear about taking Mary as your wife. It is by the Holy Spirit that she has conceived this child. She is to have a son and you are to name him Jesus because he will save his people from their sins." All this happened to fulfill what the Lord had said through the prophet:

"The virgin shall be with child
and give birth to a son,
and they shall call him Emmanuel,"

a name which means "God is with us." When Joseph awoke he did as the angel of the Lord had directed him and received her into his home as his wife. He had no relations with her at any time before she bore a son, whom he named Jesus.

THE SYNAGOGUE

Entering the Suk or public market (and avoiding the open drainage system), take the first left and then a right. Within a few steps is the entrance to the courtyard of the Melkite or Greek Catholic Church. The door at the end leads into an ancient synagogue. It is not the actual building where Jesus preached and where he had learned the Scriptures, but it is likely built on the same spot.

The Author preaching in the ancient synagogue.

Luke 4:16-30

He came to Nazareth where he had been reared, and entering the synagogue on the sabbath as he was in the habit of doing, he stood up to do the reading. When the book of the prophet Isaiah was handed him, he unrolled the scroll and found the passage where it was written:

"The spirit of the Lord is upon me;
therefore he has anointed me.
He has sent me to bring glad tidings to the poor,
to proclaim liberty to captives,
Recovery of sight to the blind and release to prisoners,
to announce a year of favor from the Lord."

Rolling up the scroll he gave it back to the assistant and sat down. All in the synagogue had their eyes fixed on him. Then he began by saying to them, "Today this Scripture passage is fulfilled in your hearing." All who were present spoke favorably of him; they marveled at the appealing discourse which came from his lips. They also asked, "Is not this Joseph's son?"

He said to them, "You will doubtless quote me the proverb, "Physician, heal yourself," and say, "Do here in your own country the things we have heard you have done in Capernaum. But in fact," he went on, "no prophet gains acceptance in his native place. Indeed, let me remind you, there were many widows in Israel in the days of Elijah when the heavens remained closed for three and a half years and a great famine spread over the land. It was to none of these that Elijah was sent, but to a widow of Zarephath near Sidon. Recall, too, the many lepers in Israel in the time of Elisha the prophet; yet not one was cured except Naaman the Syrian."

At these words the whole audience in the synagogue was filled with indignation. They rose up and expelled him from the town, leading him to the brow of the hill on which it was built and intending to hurl him over the edge. But he went straight through their midst and walked away.

Hymn
The Spirit of God Rests Upon Me (page 194)

OTHER SPOTS IN NAZARETH

The Orthodox Church of St. Gabriel has the fountain that may have been the water supply from which Jesus would have fetched jars of water for his mother. Beneath the convent of the Religieuses de Nazareth are excavations revealing an ancient tomb with a round stone to seal it. The convent of the Lebanese Poor Clares has a small building containing momentoes of Charles de Foucauld. He was their gardener in the old convent, part of which is now used by the Little Sisters of Jesus, whose rule of life he wrote. It is based upon the Nazareth life of Jesus, emphasizing prayer and manual work.

Above Nazareth is the School of the Adolescent Jesus, a trade school for boys, staffed by the Salesians of Don Bosco. It affords an unsurpassed view of Nazareth and environs, and has a lovely chapel dedicated to the adolescent Jesus.

Luke 2:51-52

> He went down with them then, and came to Nazareth, and was obedient to them. His mother meanwhile kept all these things in memory. Jesus, for his part, progressed steadily in wisdom and age and grace before God and men.

CANA

A short ride from Nazareth is the Arab village of Cana where Jesus turned water into wine. It has three churches: one Greek Orthodox, one dedicated to Nathaniel whose home was here, and the Franciscan "Wedding Church." The former two are rarely opened. The latter, across the street from a shop which sells bottles of Cana wine(!), is built on the ruins of previous Byzantine and Crusader churches.

John 2:1-11

On the third day there was a wedding at Cana in Galilee, and the mother of Jesus was there. Jesus and his disciples had likewise been invited to the celebration. At a certain point the wine ran out, and Jesus' mother told him, "They have no more wine." Jesus replied, "Woman, how does this concern of yours involve me? My hour has not yet come." His mother instructed those waiting on table, "Do whatever he tells you." As prescribed for Jewish ceremonial washings, there were at hand six stone water jars, each one holding fifteen to twenty-five gallons. "Fill those jars with water," Jesus ordered, at which they filled them to the brim. "Now," he said, "draw some out and take it to the waiter in charge." They did as he instructed them. The waiter in charge tasted the water made wine, without knowing where it had come from; only the waiters knew, since they had drawn the water. Then the waiter in charge called the groom over and remarked to him: "People usually serve the choice wine first; then when the guests have been drinking awhile, a lesser vintage. What you have done is keep the choice wine until now." Jesus performed this first of his signs at Cana in Galilee. Thus did he reveal his glory, and his disciples believed in him.

John 4:46-54

So he came again to Cana in Galilee, where he had made the water wine. And at Capernaum there was an official whose son was ill. When he heard that Jesus had come from Judea to Galilee, he went and begged him to come down and heal his son, for he was at the point of death. Jesus therefore said to him, "Unless you see signs and wonders you will not believe." The official said to him, "Sir, come down before my child dies." Jesus said to him, "Go; your son will live." The man believed the word that Jesus spoke to him and went his way. As he was going down, his servants met him and told him that his son was living. So he asked them the hour when he began to mend, and they said to him, "Yesterday at the seventh hour the fever left him." The father knew that was the hour when Jesus had said to him, "Your son will live"; and he himself believed, and all his household. This was now the second sign that Jesus did when he had come from Judea to Galilee. (R.S.V.)

This is an ideal spot for couples to renew their marriage vows.

Prayer of a Married Couple

Father, we come before you with the love for each other that you yourself have placed in our hearts. Here, your son changed water into wine. Continue to change our relationship, so that we may grow ever more deeply in love. Help us to love one another as Jesus has loved us.

In this holy place, we take each other for husband and wife again, for better, for worse, for richer, for poorer, in sickness and in health, until death do us part. Be with us, Lord, in all of our ways and strengthen us in all of our days. Amen.

Prayer for Married Couples

Father, you have given your people the blessing of marriage so that when we see a couple's love, we may learn how much you love us. Bless all married couples especially . . . May their love be a blessing on us all. Theirs is a difficult vocation in a world which gives the name love to things which are not. Be at their side, so that through the joy they have in each other, we may rejoice in you, our Loving God.

> *"Set me as a seal upon your heart*
> *as a seal on your arm;*
> *For love is strong as death*
> *jealousy as relentless as Sheol.*
> *The flash of it is a flash of fire,*
> *a flame of Yahweh himself.*
> *Love, no flood can quench,*
> *no torrents drown."*
>
> *Song of Songs 8:16 (Jerusalem Bible)*

NAIM

At the foot of Mount Tabor is the little village of Naim. Here Jesus raised the son of the poor widow from the dead.

Luke 7:11-17

> Soon afterward he went to a town called Naim, and his disciples and a large crowd accompanied him. As he approached the gate of the town a dead man was being carried out, the only son of a widowed mother. A considerable crowd of townsfolk were with her. The Lord was moved with pity upon seeing her and said to her, "Do not cry." Then he stepped forward and touched the litter; at this, the bearers halted. He said, "Young man, I bid you get up." The dead man sat up and began to speak. Then Jesus gave him back to his mother. Fear seized them all and they began to praise God. "A great prophet has risen among us," they said; and "God has visited his people." This was the report that spread about him throughout Judea and the surrounding country.

MOUNT TABOR

The Mount of the Transfiguration rises majestically above the plain. The steep road is accessible only by taxis which are usually available at the bottom. The beautiful church is surrounded by the ruins of the immense Crusader monastery of almost 1000 years ago. When the church was built about 50 years ago, the roof was of translucent alabaster, now covered over. The alabaster windows still give a sense of subdued glory. The image of the peacock in the window of the crypt (actually the ancient Byzantine Church) is symbolic of the Resurrection. The mosaic in the apse over the main altar is of the transfiguration. In the rear, incorporated into the present edifice are two ancient chapels to Moses and Elijah. Later Christians accomplished what the disciples could not: they have built three tabernacles here! The views from the observation posts at the sides of

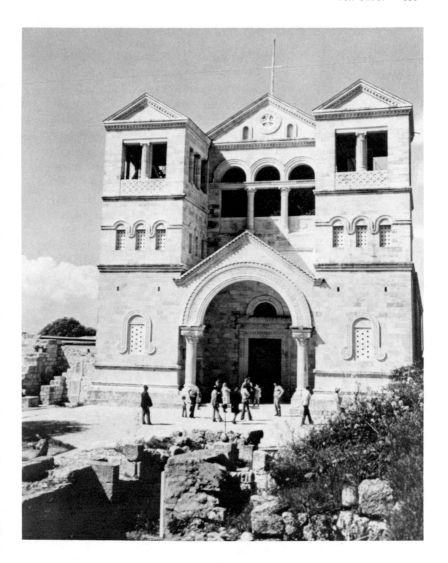

"The Basilica of the Transfiguration is surrounded by the ruins of the immense Crusader monastery of almost 1000 years ago."

the church and from the balcony of the hospice are
breathtaking.

Matthew 17:1-8

> Jesus took Peter, James, and his brother John and led
> them up on a high mountain by themselves. He was
> transfigured before their eyes. His face became as daz-
> zling as the sun, his clothes as radiant as light. Suddenly
> Moses and Elijah appeared to them conversing with him.
>
> Then Peter said to Jesus, "Lord, how good that we are
> here! With your permission I will erect three booths here,
> one for you, one for Moses, and one for Elijah." He was
> still speaking when suddenly a bright cloud overshad-
> owed them. Out of the cloud came a voice which said,
> "This is my beloved Son on whom my favor rests. Listen
> to him."

Reflection

At times it must have been depressing, being a disciple of
Jesus. To travel with him and constantly experience the
mounting hostility, the carping criticism and the negative
attitudes, could not have been encouraging.

The incident of the healing at the pool is a good example.
Jesus makes a man "whole" and the religious leaders attack
him for working on the sabbath. The opposition to him was
growing in intensity, and Jesus perceived that it was leading
him down a path of suffering.

The disciples needed a ray of hope and encouragement to
dispel the clouds of doubt. It must have been a terrible strain
to remain loyal to one whom the religious leaders declared
to be a hypocrite, a charlatan or insane.

When many had already turned off the words of Jesus,
the disciples were also tempted to do so. They desperately
needed to experience the transfiguration, and to know that
they were not wrong, even if they were very much in the
minority.

Jesus understood. Their mystical experience with him on Mount Tabor was so moving and comforting to them that they wanted to set up residence there. The beauty, calm and peace were quite a change from the antagonism they met in their ministry. They felt a deep reassurance when they perceived Jesus talking with Moses and Elijah, the real religious leaders of the people. They experienced a seal of approval on what they were about, and with renewed confidence could "listen to him."

In discouragement or disillusionment, if we go apart for prayer, and open ourselves to him, the same understanding and kindness of Jesus will come to us. He knows that we all need our moments of transfiguration, and he is waiting to touch us and say, "Rise and have no fear."

Prayer

Lord, slow us down. Sometimes we get so busy that we begin feeling sorry for ourselves and discouraged. Teach us a sense of priorities. Make us realize that if we do not go apart with you we will become empty and void. This we ask of you, Jesus, Transfigured Lord. Amen.

A MOUNTAIN IN GALILEE

St. Matthew ends his gospel with the "Great Commission" of the risen Lord to his eleven disciples. The setting is, simply, "a mountain in Galilee."

Matthew 28:16-20

> The eleven disciples made their way to Galilee, to the mountain to which Jesus has summoned them. At the sight of him, those who had entertained doubts fell down in homage. Jesus came forward and addressed them in these words:
>> "Full authority has been given to me
>> both in heaven and on earth;
>> go, therefore, and make disciples of all the nations.
>> Baptize them in the name

of the Father,
and of the Son,
and of the Holy Spirit.
Teach them to carry out everything I have
    commanded you.
And know that I am with you always,
until the end of the world!"

Hymns

How Great Thou Art (page 184)
God's Blessing Sends Us Forth (page 182)
Holy, Holy, Holy, Lord God Almighty (page 206)

SEA OF GALILEE

Jesus spent most of his ministry around the Sea of Galilee. Passing over the route that Jesus likely took from Nazareth to Capernaum one can see the double hillock of the Horns of Hattin where the Crusaders were defeated in 1187. Events in the life of Jesus that are associated with this route are the healing of a leper (Mk 1:40-45), the disciples plucking ears of grain on the sabbath, (Mk 2:23-28) and the parables of Matthew 13.

Tiberias, on the shore of the lake, was built during the lifetime of Jesus as a resort famed for its sulphur springs. From the dock of the modern town boat rides may be had up the Sea of Galilee to Capernaum. The "Sea" is about five miles wide and twelve miles long.

Luke 5:1-11

As he stood by the Lake of Gennesaret, and the crowd pressed in on him to hear the word of God, he saw two boats moored by the side of the lake; the fishermen had disembarked and were washing their nets. He got into one of the boats, the one belonging to Simon, and asked him to pull out a short distance from the shore; then, remaining seated, he continued to teach the crowds from the boat. When he had finished speaking he said to

Simon, "Put out into deep water and lower your nets for a catch." Simon answered, "Master, we have been hard at it all night long and have caught nothing; but if you say so, I will lower the nets."

Upon doing this they caught such a great number of fish that their nets were at the breaking point. They signaled to their mates in the other boat to come and help them. These came, and together they filled the two boats until they nearly sank.

At the sight of this, Simon Peter fell at the knees of Jesus saying, "Leave me, Lord, I am a sinful man." For indeed, amazement at the catch they had made seized him and all his shipmates, as well as James and John, Zebedee's sons, who were partners with Simon. Jesus said to Simon, "Do not be afraid. From now on you will be catching men." With that they brought their boats to land, left everything, and became his followers.

Mark 4:35-41

That day as evening drew on he said to them, "Let us cross over to the farther shore." Leaving the crowd, they took him away in the boat in which he was sitting, while the other boats accompanied him. It happened that a bad squall blew up. The waves were breaking over the boat and it began to ship water badly. Jesus was in the stern through it all, sound asleep on a cushion. They finally woke him and said to him, "Teacher, does it not matter to you that we are going to drown?" He awoke and rebuked the wind and said to the sea: "Quiet! Be still!" The wind fell off and everything grew calm. Then he said to them, "Why are you lacking in faith?" A great awe overcame them at this. They kept saying to one another, "Who can this be that the wind and the sea obey him?"

Matthew 14:22-33

Immediately afterward, while dismissing the crowds, Jesus insisted that his disciples get into the boat and precede him to the other side. When he had sent them away, he went up on the mountain by himself to pray, remaining there alone as evening drew on. Meanwhile the boat, already several hundred yards out from shore, was being tossed about in the waves raised by strong head-winds. At about three in the morning, he came walking toward them on the lake. When the disciples saw him walking on the water, they were terrified. "It is a ghost!" They said, and in their fear they began to cry out. Jesus hastened to reassure them: "Get hold of yourselves! It is I. Do not be afraid!" Peter spoke up and said, "Lord, if it is really you, tell me to come to you across the water." "Come!" he said. So Peter got out of the boat and began to walk on the water, moving toward Jesus. But when he perceived how strong the wind was, becoming frightened, he began to sink and cried out, "Lord, save me!" Jesus at once stretched out his hand and caught him. "How little faith you have!" he exclaimed. "Why did you falter?" Once they had climbed into the boat, the wind died down. Those who were in the boat showed him reverence, declaring, "Beyond doubt you are the Son of God!"

There Are Two Seas
A Parable by Bruce Barton

There are two seas in Palestine. One is fresh, and fish are in it. Splashes of green adorn its banks. Trees spread their branches over it, and stretch out their thirsty roots to dip of its healing water. Along its shore the children play.

The River Jordan makes this sea with sparkling water from the hills. So it laughs in the sunshine. And men build their houses near to it, and birds their nests; and every kind of life is happier because it is there.

The River Jordan flows on south into another sea. Here is no splash of fish, no fluttering leaf, no song of birds, no children's laughter. Travellers choose another route, unless on urgent business. The air hangs above its waters and neither man nor beast nor fowl will drink. What makes this mighty difference in these neighbor seas? Not the River Jordan. It empties the same good water into both. Not the soil in which they lie; not the country round about.

This is the difference. The Sea of Galilee receives but does not keep the Jordan. For every drop that flows into it another drop flows out. The giving and receiving go on in equal measure. The other sea is shrewder, hoarding its income jealously. It will not be tempted into any generous impulse. Every drop it gets, it keeps. The Sea of Galilee gives and lives. This other sea gives nothing. It is named the Dead.
There are two seas in Palestine.
There are two kinds of people in the world.
Which kind are we?

Hymns
How Great Thou Art (page 184)
A Mighty Fortress (page 174)

CAPERNAUM

THE SYNAGOGUE

This was Jesus' favorite town, and he considered it home. Here he preached in the synagogue and here he gathered his disciples. The excavations carried out by the Franciscans in recent yearts have uncovered a good bit of the early town.

The synagogue is believed to be of the fifth century A.D. The splendid structure was obviously built by wealthy Jews who took lightly the ban on making images. Acanthus, pomagranates, Roman eagles and even the ark of the covenant were carved into the stone. Some were effaced by a later, more orthodox generation. The synagogue where Jesus preached very likely had stood on the same spot. The Jews sent by the centurion pleaded: "He deserves this favor from you, because he loves our people and even built a synagogue for us" (Lk 7:5).

A detail from the synagogue

Mark 3:1-6

 He returned to the synagogue where there was a man
whose hand was shriveled up. They kept an eye on Jesus
to see whether he would heal him on the sabbath, hoping
to be able to bring an accusation against him. He
addressed the man with the shriveled hand: "Stand up
here in front!" Then he said to them: "Is it permitted to do
a good deed on the sabbath — or an evil one? To preserve
life or to destroy it?" At this they remained silent. He
looked around at them with anger, for he was deeply
grieved that they had closed their minds against him.

Then he said to the man, "Stretch out your hand." The man did so and his hand was perfectly restored. When the Pharisees went outside, they immediately began to plot with the Herodians how they might destroy him.

John 6:26-59

When they found him on the other side of the lake, they said to him, "Rabbi, when did you come here?" Jesus answered them:

"I assure you,
you are not looking for me because you have seen signs but because you have eaten your fill of the loaves. You should not be working for perishable food but for food that remains unto life eternal, food which the Son of Man will give you; it is on him that God the Father has set his seal."

At this they said to him, "What must we do to perform the works of God?" Jesus replied:

"This is the work of God:
have faith in the One whom he sent."

"So that we can put faith in you," they asked him, "what sign are you going to perform for us to see? What is the 'work' you do? Our ancestors had manna to eat in the desert; according to Scripture, 'He gave them bread from the heavens to eat.'" Jesus said to them:

"I solemnly assure you,
it was not Moses who gave you bread from the heavens it is my Father who gives you the real heavenly bread. God's bread comes down from heaven and gives life to the world."

"Sir, give us this bread always," they besought him. Jesus explained to them:

"I myself am the bread of life.
No one who comes to me shall ever be hungry, no one who believes in me shall ever thirst.
But as I told you —
though you have seen me, you still do not believe.
All that the Father gives me shall come to me;

no one who comes will I ever reject,
because it is not to do my own will
that I have come down from heaven,
but to do the will of him who sent me.
It is the will of him who sent me
that I should lose nothing of what he has given me;
rather, that I should raise it up on the last day.
Indeed, this is the will of my Father,
that everyone who looks upon the Son
and believes in him
shall have eternal life.
Them I will raise up on the last day."

At this the Jews started to murmur in protest because he claimed, "I am the bread that came down from heaven." They kept saying: "Is this not Jesus, the son of Joseph? Do we not know his father and mother? How can he claim to have come down from heaven?" "Stop your murmuring," Jesus told them.

"No one can come to me
unless the Father who sent me draws him;
I will raise him up on the last day.
It is written in the prophets:
'They shall all be taught by God.'
Everyone who has heard the Father
and learned from him comes to me.
Not that anyone has seen the Father —
only the one who is from God has seen the Father.
Let me firmly assure you,
whoever believes has eternal life.
Your ancestors ate manna in the desert,
    but they died.
This is the bread that comes down from heaven
for one to eat and never die.
I myself am the living bread
come down from heaven.
If anyone eats this bread they shall live forever;
the bread I will give is my flesh,
for the life of the world."

At this the Jews quarreled among themselves saying,

"How can he give us his flesh to eat?" Thereupon Jesus said to them:

> "Let me solemnly assure you,
> if you do not eat the flesh of the Son of Man
> and drink his blood,
> you have no life in you.
> whoever feeds on my flesh and drinks my blood
> has life eternal, and I will raise them up on the
>   last day.
> For my flesh is real food
> and my blood real drink.
> The one who feeds on my flesh
> and drinks my blood
> remains in me, and I in them.
> Just as the Father who has life sent me
> and I have life because of the Father,
> so the one who feeds on me
> will have life because of me.
> This is the bread that came down from heaven.
> Unlike your ancestors who ate and died nonetheless,
> the one who feeds on this bread shall live forever."

He said this in a synagogue instruction at Capernaum.

Reflection

Capernaum was Jesus' favorite city. "A prophet is without honor in his own country" was all too tragically true of Nazareth. Driven from there with hostility and threats of death, Jesus was fond of Capernaum on the Sea of Galilee. No more than we could Jesus take rejection — much less callous indifference.

He shook the dust of Nazareth from his sandals and went where people were open enough to listen to his words. The fact that the early Christians remembered such an insignificant spot as the home of Peter's mother-in-law and erected upon it a church-synagogue shows that they too, after the destruction of Jerusalem, found this a hospitable town. Synagogues were the center for prayer and hearing the Word of God in each community. Sacrifice was limited to the Temple in Jerusalem, 75 miles away. Thus the synagogue was the focus of the spiritual life, except for the pilgrim feasts which brought one to Jerusalem.

Never before had the citizens of Capernaum heard such words full of spirit and life. They came forth, not from written Torah scroll, but from the very word of God himself. They were the words that held out the hope and the promise of Eternal life.

In the breaking of the bread, the Eucharist, we are offered life, life such as we could never have imagined or striven for. It is the very sharing in the life of Jesus himself. And because it is the flesh and blood of the Risen Lord, it is a foretaste of our own resurrection.

The words that Jesus spoke at Capernaum, promising life eternal, are the words that come true each time we gather as a Christian community. We are the living fulfillment of his promise. Capernaum with its synagogue has fallen into ruins. His word endures forever, and because of what he said here, we shall live forever.

Prayer

Father, we know that we, though many, are one body for we all partake of the same bread. We cannot fathom the mystery, but we will not go away, for your Son has the word of eternal life. Help us to work for the external manifestation of that Unity which your Son has already accomplished in us. Help us to accomplish the prayer of Jesus that all may be one as you and he are one. This we ask through Christ Our Lord. Amen.

Hymns

I am the Bread of Life (page 185)
Let Us Break Bread Together. (page 186)

PETER'S HOUSE

Not far from the synagogue is the Byzantine octagonal church and sacristy. Graffiti on the stones of the earlier levels indicate that this was venerated as a sacred spot, very likely as the home of Peter and his family, where Jesus stayed.

Mark 1:29-33

Immediately upon leaving the synagogue, he entered the house of Simon and Andrew with James and John. Simon's mother-in-law lay ill with a fever, and the first thing they did was to tell him about her. He went over to her and grasped her hand and helped her up, and the fever left her. She immediately began to wait on them.

After sunset, as evening drew on, they brought him all who were ill, and those possessed by demons. Before long the whole town was gathered outside the door.

Mark 2:1-12

He came back to Capernaum after a lapse of several days and word got around that he was at home. At that they began to gather in great numbers. There was no longer any room for them, even around the door. While he was delivering God's word to them, some people arrived bringing a paralyzed man to him. The four who carred him were unable to bring him to Jesus because of the crowd, so they began to open up the roof over the spot where Jesus was. When they had made a hole, they let down the mat on which the paralytic was lying. When Jesus saw their faith, he said to the paralyzed man, "My son, your sins are forgiven." Now some of the scribes were sitting there asking themselves: "Why does the man talk in that way? He commits blasphemy! Who can forgive sins except God alone?" Jesus was immediately aware of their reasoning, though they kept it to themselves, and he said to them: "Why do you harbor these thoughts? Which is easier, to say to the paralytic, 'Your sins are forgiven,' or to say, 'Stand up, pick up your mat, and walk again'? That you may know that the Son of Man has authority on earth to forgive sins," (he said to the paralyzed man) "I command you: Stand up! Pick up your mat and go home." The man stood and picked up his mat and went outside in the sight of everyone. They were awestruck; all gave praise to God saying "We have never seen anything like this!"

Matthew 11:20-24

He began to reproach the towns where most of his miracles had been worked, with their failure to reform: "It will go ill with you, Chorazin! And just as ill with you, Bethsaida! If the miracles worked in you had taken place in Tyre and Sidon, they would have reformed in sackcloth and ashes long ago. I assure you, it will go easier for Tyre and Sidon than for you on the day of judgment. As for you, Capernaum,

'Are you to be exalted to the skies?
You shall go down to the realm of death!'

If the miracles worked in you had taken place in Sodom, it would be standing today. I assure you, it will go easier for Sodom than for you on the day of judgment."

Matthew 17:24-27

When they entered Capernaum, the collectors of the temple tax approached Peter and said, "Does your master not pay the temple tax?" "Of course he does," Peter replied. Then Jesus on entering the house asked, without giving him time to speak: "What is your opinion, Simon? Do the kings of the world take tax or toll from their sons, or from foreigners?" When he replied, "From foreigners," Jesus observed: "Then their sons are exempt. But for fear of disedifying them go to the lake, throw in a line, and take out the first fish you catch. Open its mouth and you will discover there a coin worth twice the temple tax. Take it and give it to them for you and me."

It would seem that "Peter's House" stood near the business center of the town. Here, too, the taxes would be collected.

Matthew 9:9-15

As he moved on, Jesus saw a man named Matthew at his post where taxes were collected. He said to him,

"Follow me." Matthew got up and followed him. Now it happened that while Jesus was at table in Matthew's home, many tax collectors and those known as sinners came to join Jesus and his disciples at dinner. The Pharisees saw this and complained to his disciples, "What reason can the Teacher have for eating with tax collectors and those who disregard the law?" Overhearing the remark, he said: "People who are in good health do not need a doctor; sick people do. Go and learn the meaning of the words, 'It is mercy I desire and not sacrifice.' I have come to call, not the self-righteous, but sinners."

The garden opposite the friary at the exit has a statue of St. Francis reaching out to "brother sun and sister moon," sculpted by Father Martini, O.F.M., who is also responsible for the artistic work in the Chapel of Cenacle, the Chapel of the Apparition in the Holy Sepulchre and at the following holy place.

TABGHA

South of Capernaum is the newly renovated chapel built over a rock commemorating the primacy of Peter. (Caesarea Philippi of Matthew 16 is quite a bit north at Banias, the source of the Jordan.) Here on the lake shore Jesus appeared to his disciples after the resurrection and singled out Peter to feed his sheep. The newly-built outdoor ecumenical sanctuary and garden overlooking the water are a perfect setting for meditating on the mystery of the Church. The newly erected bronze of Jesus and Peter is also by Father Martini, O.F.M.

John 21:1-17

Later, at the Sea of Tiberias, Jesus showed himself to the disciples (once again). This is how the appearance took place. Assembled were Simon Peter, Thomas ("the Twin), Nathanael (from Cana in Galiliee), Zebedee's sons, and two other disciples. Simon Peter said to them, "I am going out to fish." "We will join you," they replied, and went off to get into their boat. All through the night they caught nothing. Just after daybreak Jesus was standing on the shore, though none of the disciples knew it was Jesus. He said to them, "Children, have you caught anything to eat?" "Not a thing," they answered. "Cast your net off to the starboard side," he suggested, "and you will find something." So they made a cast, and took so many fish they could not haul the net in. Then the disciple Jesus loved cried out to Peter, "It is the Lord!" On hearing it was the Lord, Simon Peter threw on some clothes — he was stripped — and jumped into the water.

Meanwhile, the other disciples came in the boat, towing the net full of fish. Actually they were not far from land — no more than a hundred yards.

When they landed, they saw a charcoal fire there with a fish laid on it and some bread. "Bring some of the fish you just caught," Jesus told them. Simon Peter went aboard and hauled ashore the net loaded with sizable fish — one hundred fifty-three of them! In spite of the great number, the net was not torn.

"Come and eat your meal," Jesus told them. Not one of the disciples presumed to inquire, "Who are you?" for they knew it was the Lord. Jesus came over, took the bread and gave it to them, and did the same with the fish. This marked the third time that Jesus appeared to the disciples after being raised from the dead.

When they had eaten their meal, Jesus said to Simon Peter, "Simon, son of John, do you love me more than these?" "Yes, Lord," he said, "you know that I love you." At which Jesus said, "Feed my lambs."

A second time he put his question, "Simon, son of John, do you love me?" Peter said "Yes, Lord, you know that I love you." Jesus replied, "Tend my sheep."

A third time Jesus asked him, "Simon, son of John, do

you love me?" Peter was hurt because he had asked a third time, "Do you love me?" So he said to him: "Lord, you know everything. You know well that I love you." Jesus said to him, "Feed my sheep."

Hymn
The Church's One Foundation (page 177)

Ancient mosaic of loaves and fishes, incorporated into the sanctuary floor of the Benedictine Church.

THE MULTIPLICATION OF LOAVES

The adjoining property in the care of the Benedictines is the site of the recently built basilica of the Loaves and Fishes. It was constructed to mark the traditional spot of that episode, but also to preserve the fourth-century mosaic from the Byzantine church, depicting the miracle of the loaves and fishes, as well as much of the flora and fauna of Palestine.

Mark 6:30-44

The apostles returned to Jesus and reported to him all that they had done and what they had taught. He said to them, "Come by yourselves to an out-of-the-way place and rest a little." People were coming and going in great numbers, making it impossible for them to so much as eat. So Jesus and the apostles went off in the boat by themselves to a deserted place. People saw them leaving, and many got to know about it. People from all the towns hastened on foot to the place, arriving ahead of them.

Upon disembarking Jesus saw a vast crowd. He pitied them, for they were like sheep without a shepherd; and he began to teach them at great length. It was now getting late and his disciples came to him with a suggestion: "This is a deserted place and it is already late. Why do you not dismiss them so that they can go to the crossroads and villages around here and buy themselves something to eat?" "You give them something to eat," Jesus replied. At that they said, "Are we to go and spend two hundred days' wages for bread to feed them?" "How many loaves have you?" Jesus asked. "Go and see." When they learned the number they answered, "Five, and two fish." He told them to make the people sit down on the green grass in groups or parties. The people took their places in hundreds and fifties, neatly arranged like flower beds. Then, taking the five loaves and the two fish, Jesus raised his eyes to heaven, pronounced a blessing, broke the loaves, and gave them to the disciples to distribute. He divided the two fish among all of them and they ate until they had their fill. They gathered up enough leftovers to fill twelve baskets, besides what remained of the fish. Those who had eaten the loaves numbered five thousand men.

Reflection

What a strange thing for Jesus to say: "You give them something to eat." He knew better than the disciples that they had nothing to offer to the people. It almost seems as if he is playing a game with them: "You, from your own resources, you take care of their needs." This could only lead to a sense of frustration and helplessness on the part of the disciples.

If they had tried to divide their meager resources, a postage stamp would have been too large a platter for the meal they would have been able to serve each one! They had to admit helplessness and defeat: "We have nothing. Five loaves and two fishes are nothing for feeding five thousand men, plus women and children."

Try it sometime. Try catering a banquet, even for ten, with a loaf of bread and a can of sardines.

The people present got something out of this episode; a free meal. But, they missed the point. Afterward, one can almost hear the tragic disappointment in Jesus' voice as he says to them: "Truly, truly, I say to you, you seek me, not because you saw signs, but because you ate your fill of the loaves. Do not labor for the food which perishes, but for the food which endures to eternal life, which the Son of Man will give you, for on him, God the Father has set his seal . . . After this many of his disciples drew back, and no longer went about with him" (Jn 6:26 and 66).

Those who continued to remain with him, however, got a great deal from this episode. These disciples learned in a dramatic way that if they were going to be effective, it would not be from their own resources but because of the power of Jesus within them. Their frustration led them to a deeper faith, knowing that without him their efforts were futile. So are ours! "I am the vine, you are the branches. He who abides in me, and I in him, he it is that bears much fruit, for apart from me you can do nothing" (Jn 15:5).

Prayer
O thou who clothest the lilies
and feedest the birds of the air,
Who leadest the lambs to pasture
and the hart to the water's side.

Who has multiplied loaves and fishes
and converted water to wine,
Do thou come to our table
as giver and guest to dine. Amen.

Hymn
Let Us Break Together (page 186)

MOUNT OF BEATITUDES

Atop the mountain overlooking the Sea of Galilee and across from the Golan Heights are the chapel and hospice of the Italian Franciscan Sisters. Matthew has here gathered into one sermon the teaching of Jesus. If time permits, the whole sermon of Matthew 5-7 should be read.

Matthew 5:1-16

When he saw the crowds he went up on the mountainside. After he had sat down his disciples gathered around him, and he began to teach them:

"How blest are the poor in spirit;
the reign of God is theirs.
Blest too are the sorrowing, they shall be consoled.
(Blest are the lowly; they shall inherit the land)
Blest are they who hunger and thirst for holiness;
they shall have their fill.
Blest are they who show mercy;
mercy shall be theirs.
Blest are the single-hearted
for they shall see God.
Blest too the peacemakers; they shall be called
the children of God.
Blest are those persecuted for holiness sake;
the reign of God is theirs.
Blest are you when they insult you and persecute you
and utter every kind of slander against you
because of me.
Be glad and rejoice, for your reward is great in
heaven;
they persecuted the prophets before you in the
very same way.

"You are the salt of the earth. But what if salt goes flat? How can you restore its flavor? Then it is good for nothing but to be thrown out and trampled underfoot.

"You are the light of the world. A city set on a hill cannot be hidden. People do not light a lamp and then put it under a bushel basket. They set it on a stand where it gives light to all in the house. In the same way, your light must shine before all so that they may see goodness in your acts and give praise to your heavenly Father."

Reflection

Moses received the commandments for God's covenanted people on a mountain. The people and priests were warned not to come close, lest they die. And they trembled at the fire, lightning, clouds and noise that accompanied the event.

When Jesus goes beyond the commandments and gives the Sermon on the Mount, the contrast is startling. The disciples go up to the mountain with him, to this spot of unsurpassed beauty, looking over the Sea of Galilee. In calmness and gentleness, they hear not threats of death, but words of life. Jesus, realizing that the Law has run its course, because it can only guide external behavior, tries to get into their hearts and change them from within.

To be "Blessed" is to live in such a way so that others can see the reality of God and the power of his love in us.

The Poor in Spirit are those whose lives are not cluttered and possessed and are therefore open to God and his kingdom.

Those who mourn are not those who attend wakes, but rather those who are genuinely disturbed when they perceive that Love is not loved.

The Meek are not those who would allow themselves to be walked upon, but are those who would walk anywhere to bring the gentleness of God.

Those who hunger and thirst for righteousness are those for whom right relationship with God is more satisfying than food and drink.

The Merciful are those who have experienced God's love

and know how to share it with others.

The Pure in Heart are those with a one-track mind, who have a sense of priorities with the chief priority being God.

The Peacemakers are those who do what Jesus came to do, breaking down those barriers that keep us from being whole (Shalom) and which separate us from each other.

Laws can never accomplish these things. Only Jesus, the Light of the World, shining within us, can.

Prayer
Lord Jesus, your words are a call to maturity in your gospel. So often we are content with performing the minimum and what is external. Enter our hearts and stir them to respond to you totally. Grant that we be blessed because our lives have been living editions of your gospel. Amen.

Hymns
Whatsoever You Do (page 201)
How Great Thou Art (page 184)
Battle Hymn of the Republic (page 208)

BAPTISM IN THE JORDAN

Just below the spot where the Sea of Galilee empties its water into the gentle Jordan a kibbutz has provided facilities for conveniently entering the waters for renewal of Baptismal Vows. Exactly where John baptized Jesus is not known. The chapel on the bank of the river near Jericho is presently off limits for reasons of military security.

Matthew 3:13-17

Jesus, coming from Galilee, appeared before John at the Jordan to be baptized by him. John tried to refuse him with the protest, "I should be baptized by you, yet you come to me!" Jesus answered: "Give in for now. We must do this if we would fulfill all of God's demands." So he came directly out of the water. Suddenly the sky

*The author renewing baptismal
commitment in the Jordan River*

opened and he saw the Spirit of God descend like a dove
and hover over him. With that, a voice from the heavens
said, "This is my beloved Son. My favor rests on him."

Reflection

The Jordan is a small river, not much more than a creek
by our standards. Its gentle waters flow from the lively Sea
of Galilee into the Dead Sea. It is the channel between life
and death. Along its banks vegetation flourishes, and its
waters teem with aquatic life.

Never before this moment, however, were they so full of
life ... The Way, the Truth and the Life stands in them to be
baptized by John. Always a sign of life and growth, in this
moment, so startling and pregnant with hope, these waters
become a foretaste of rebirth and eternal life. Jesus became
like us in everything except sin, so he does not need this

Baptism. He enters the water not for his own sake, but for ours.

This baptism of John's is a figure of the one that Jesus will give, imparting the Spirit, but that must wait for his dying and rising. "Do you not know that all of us who have been baptized into Christ Jesus were baptized into his death? We were buried therefore with him by baptism into death, so that as Christ was raised from the dead by the glory of the Father, we too might walk in newness of life" (Rom 6:3).

In Jesus' Baptism unto discipleship, we become one with him. We become the Body of Christ. We can call God "Abba" — Father. We are made a new creation. We come to a new birth in water and the Holy Spirit. The Holy Spirit dwells in our hearts. We become the temple of God. We become more closely related than if we were blood brothers and sisters.

Because of what Jesus has accomplished, we are sealed by the Holy Spirit as God's own possession and he is given to us as a pledge of future glory. If those waters of the Jordan had ears they would hear God saying of us, the brothers and sisters of Christ: "This is my beloved." And the waves would rise in chorus to proclaim: "There is one Lord, one faith, one Baptism, one God who is Father."

Renewal of Baptismal Commitment

Father, at the waters where the Spirit descended upon your beloved Son, I promise...

> *To confess Jesus as Lord by word and life.*
> *To abide in him in whom alone I can bear much fruit.*
> *To live his holy gospel.*
> *To do for the least of his brethren whatever I can.*
> *To avoid whatever would distract or withdraw*
> *me from the good shepherd of my soul.*
> *To call upon you whom Jesus revealed as Abba.*
> *Our Father...*

Hymn
There Is One Lord   (page 196)
Come Holy Ghost   (page 180)
Michael, Row the Boat Ashore   (page 207)
Swing Low Sweet Chariot   (page 207)

THE MEDITERRANEAN COAST

Apart from a surprising mention of Jesus going to Tyre and Sidon (Mk 7:20) there is no suggestion that Jesus spent any time on the coast. However, Acco was the Crusader port, and stronghold, and Mount Carmel is noted for Elijah's contest with the prophets of Baal (1 Kgs 18). Further south, Herod's city of Caesarea was the scene of the trial of Paul (Acts 23-26) and Peter's visit with Cornelius (Acts 10:23-48). Peter's vision took place in Jaffa [Joppa] (Acts 10:9-23).

Prayer at the End of a Pilgrimage

Father, we have walked in the land where Jesus walked. We have touched the soil and rocks where the seed falls. We have seen the lilies of the field and heard the birds of the air.

We have been warmed by the sun that warmed him and cooled by the breezes that touched his face. We have been to the sea where he walked, and to the river where he was baptized. We have felt the presence of the Holy Spirit where he first sent it, and anguished at the spot where he gave himself for us.

We have rejoiced at the emptiness of his tomb and the fullness of his love in our hearts.

Be with us as we continue our earthly pilgrimage to the New Jerusalem where every tear will be wiped away and we will be with you, your Son and the Holy Spirit forever. AMEN.

"If I forget you, O Jerusalem,
  May my right hand be forgotten."
                                    Ps. 137:5

APPENDICES

The Peoples of the Holy Land

ARABS

The Arabian peninsula was the original home of the Arabs who speak a Semitic language. The Bible recognizes them as the descendants of Esau, brother of Jacob and son of Abraham. Most, though not all, adopted the Moslem religion. Whether Christian or Moslem they venerate Abraham as El Khalil, the friend of God. By the seventh century they had arrived in Jerusalem.

ARMENIANS

These are the peoples from around the Caspian Sea (present-day Russia and Turkey) who embraced Christianity in the third century. Within a couple of centuries there was a significant group that came to Jerusalem and they have had a continuous presence ever since. In their native land, they were victims of a terrible genocide earlier in this century. Their Patriarch is considered the successor of St. James, Bishop of Jerusalem (Acts 15:13ff). The cathedral is open during vespers in the mid-afternoon. The Armenian Quarter is found between the Jaffa and the Zion gates.

DRUSE

A Moslem sect inhabiting parts of Syria, Lebanon and Israel. Their religious practices are secret but it is known that they gather once a year to honor Jethro, the father-in-law of Moses. Having suffered as schismatics at the hands of other Moslems, many of them are supportive of the State of Israel and are permitted to serve in the armed forces.

FRANCISCANS
(Order of Friars Minor)

In 1217 Friars first came to the Holy Land with their founder, St. Francis of Assisi. They are and have been for centuries the official custodians of the holy places. In addition they run parishes, ophanages, schools, hospitals, ecumenical centers, museums, a Biblical School, etc. They number almost 400 and come from 22 countries. The Custos of the Holy Land who is also called the Guardian of Mount Zion has his headquarters at St. Savior convent on St. Francis Street in the Christian quarter, near the New Gate.

JEWS

Technically the Jews are the descendents of one tribe of Israel, Juda, that survived after the deportation of the ten tribes of the North in 721 B.C. The Cohens (Priests) and Levis (Levites) are from the tribe of Levi which did not have a portion in the land.

Those who survived the evil and despicable plan of Hitler in the Holocaust are divided into three major religious affiliations. The orthodox adhere strictly to the Torah. The strictest of them are the Hassidim (Pious Ones) who frequently wear the clothing of their native villages in seventeenth-century Poland and Russia. A small minority oppose the existence of the State of Israel as being a blasphemous effort to force the hand of God. Like most orthodox they tend to prefer a ghetto like Mea Sharim where they can practice their religion faithfully without danger of contamination.

Conservative and Reform Jewry are efforts to come to grips with contemporary life and still be religious. A very large percentage of Israelis are culturally and ethnically Jews, but shun any religious affiliation.

MELKITES OR GREEK CATHOLICS

They take their name from Melek (king) since they sided with the emperor in a time of heresy. They are mainly from Syria and are in union with Rome. There are a number of Arabs who are Greek Catholic and in addition to their Patriachate in Jerusalem, they have an Archdiocese in Galilee.

MARONITES

These are uniates or Eastern Rite Catholics in union with Rome. They are mostly of Lebanese origin and use Aramaic, the language of Jesus, in their liturgy. They take their name from St. Maron. They are represented in Jerusalem at their Patriarchal Vicariate and hospice, behind the Christian Information Center near Jaffa Gate.

MOSLEMS

The peoples, many but not all of whom are Arabs, who follow the Prophet Mohammed. Six times a day the call to prayer can be heard from their mosques. Their sacred book is the Koran. They believe that the Prophet came to Jerusalem and ascended into heaven from the rock where the Dome of the Rock now stands. They honor Mary, Jesus,

Moses and Abraham. They have no priesthood and are divided into many sects. Their name for Jerusalem is El Quds, The Holy.

ORTHODOX

This is the designation of those autonomous churches that in the course of history have severed their ties with Rome. They are distinguished one from another by the countries in which they are most predominant. The Greek Orthodox are the most numerous of the auto-cephalous (independent with their own patriarch) churches that are represented in Jerusalem. The Armenians are strong. The Russians are divided into red or white, based upon whether or not they are in union with the Moscow Patriarchate. Among the smaller groups are the Syrian, Coptic (Egyptian) and Ethiopian. Many of them have counterparts among the Roman Catholics, who have returned to union with Rome, but retain their own distinctive ritual, language and culture.

PATRIARCHS

Abraham, Isaac and Jacob are the patriarchs through whom God made his covenant with his people.

In Christian times patriarchs are usually considered the successor to an apostle in a church established by one. The Pope is the patriarch of the West as Bishop of Peter's Church of Rome. The Orthodox Patriarch of the East at Istanbul is the successor of St. Andrew. In Jerusalem, the major Christian churches each have a patriarch, and in the Christian Quarter the roads that lead to or past their residences are designated Greek Catholic Patriarchate Road, Latin Catholic Patriarchate Road, etc.

PALESTINIANS

Before the establishment of the State of Israel in 1948, the area between the Jordan and the Mediterranean was known as Palestine (after Philistine, early inhabitants of the coastal plain). Many modern inhabitants fled to the "West Bank" in the 1948 War of Independence. Many also fled to Jordan, Lebanon and other Arab countries. Another exodus took place in the 1967 war, mostly to Lebanon. Thus, today, there are Palestinians who live in Israel, the occupied territories, and the Arab countries as well as in Europe and North America.

SAMARITANS

These are the descendants of the ten tribes of the Northern Kingdom of Israel. When the majority of them were deported in 721 B.C., the remainder intermarried with pagans. Since their break from the tribe of Juda came long before the Bible was completed, they accept only the Pentateuch or first five books of Moses. Their center is in Nablus, where the high priest leads them in sacrifice. There are less than 500 in the world.

Items of Interest

This sign, the abbreviation for *Taphos* (Gr. Tomb), is the mark of the Greek Orthodox and is to be found on property controlled by them.

The Crusader or Jerusalem Cross is the mark of the Franciscan Custody of the Holy Land. Its origin is unknown but it is said to signify either the five countries that came on the crusades, or the five wounds of Christ. It marks the places in the care of the Franciscans.

ISRAELI TOURIST OFFICE

Just inside Jaffa Gate, to the left, the government tourist office provides maps, schedules and a wealth of information about events in Jerusalem.

CHRISTIAN INFORMATION CENTER

Inside Jaffa Gate, turn to the right. Immediately on the left is the Pilgrim Center conducted by the Franciscan Custody of the Holy Land. Only here can arrangements be made for celebrating liturgy at the Holy Places. For those on a religious pilgrimage, they will also issue, given sufficient notice, a beautifully illuminated certificate of pilgrimage with your name on it. Guidebooks, pamphlets and notices of events are also available.

ROCKEFELLER MUSEUM

Open: 10 a.m.-6 p.m.; Fridays and Saturdays to 2 p.m. Established in 1927, this museum is exclusively archaeological. The exhibits, running from the Stone Age to the C18, are arranged chronologically.

BOOKSTORES

One can hardly begin the Via Dolorosa without a half-dozen young Arab entrepreneurs clamoring to sell guidebooks, postcards and such pictorial souvenir books as those so beautifully done by Fr. Wolfgang Pax, O.F.M., Professor at the Franciscan Biblical School at the First Station.

In addition to this book store of the streets, the gift shop at the Ecce Homo Convent of the Sisters of Zion offers a fine selection of books. It is also unique in offering not only sets of slides, but individual ones as well. The St. Francis Bookshop on St. Francis Street near the New Gate offers a rich choice of books in addition to Guidebooks; Archaeological, Spiritual, Theological and Biblical books are available in several languages.

For Further Reading

GUIDES

Hoade, O.F.M., Eugene, *Guide to the Holy Land*, Franciscan Printing Press, Jerusalem. (A very detailed and complete guide)

Bishco, Herbert. *This is Jerusalem. A Complete Walkabout Guidebook*. Heritage Publishing Co., Tel Aviv. 1981 (A good concise book for the pocket.)

Richards, Hubert J. *Pilgrim to the Holy Land*, a practical guide, Mayhew McCrinmon, Great Wakering, Essex, England. 1982. (Excellent, up-to-date and complete, written by an expert especially for English and Irish pilgrims.)

ARCHAEOLOGY

Cornfeld, Gallyah and Freedman, David Noel, *Archaeology of the Bible, Book by Book*. Harper and Row, San Francisco. (Well illustrated with plenty of maps. A fine resource)

Harker, Ronald. *Digging Up the Bible Lands*. Henry Y. Walck, Inc., N.Y. (Easy reading with many illustrations, ... some in color)

Murphy-O'Connor, Jerome O.P. *The Holy Land, An Archaeological Guide*, from earliest times to 1770. Oxford University Press, N.Y. 1980. (A splendid guide written by an expert with a sense of humor. He is professor at the Ecole Biblique in Jerusalem. It is the result of his tours guiding U.N. personnel.)

Wilkinson, John, *Jerusalem As Jesus Knew It. Archaeology As Evidence*, Thames and Hudson, London, 1978. (The title is a bit misleading. The author does not try to prove that the Bible is true. However, he does bring to life the sites linked to the life of Jesus.)

PERIODICALS

Biblical Archaeology Review, 3111 Rittenhouse Street, N.W., Washington, D.C. 20015. (A fine magazine, well written and beautifully illustrated that keeps you up-to-date on all the new discoveries. $22.50 per year for six issues.)

Holy Land, illustrated quarterly of the Franciscan Custody of the Holy Land, 1400 Quincy St., N.E., Washington, D.C. 20017. (Just recently made available in North America, it contains enlightening articles on the history and archaeology of the Holy Land. $6.00 per year.)

National Geographic, P.O. Box 2895, Washington, D.C. 20013. (Frequently contains articles of interest to lovers of the Holy Land, e.g., "This Year in Jerusalem," by Joseph Judge, April, 1983. It is worth going through the index for the last twenty years. $15.00 per year)

🌿 A Final Reflection

"And now God says to us what he has already said to the world as a whole through his grace-filled birth: 'I am there. I am with you. I am your life. I am your time. I am the gloom of your daily routine. Why will you not bear it? I weep your tears — pour out yours to me, my child. I am your joy. Do not be afraid to be happy, for ever since I wept, joy is the standard of living that is really more suitable than the anxiety and grief of those who think they have no hope. I am the blind alleys of all your paths, for when you no longer know how to go any farther, then you have reached me, foolish child, though you are not aware of it. I am in your anxiety, for I have shared it by suffering it. And in doing so, I wasn't even heroic according to the wisdom of the world. I am in the prison of your finiteness, for my love has made me your prisoner. When the totals of your plans and of your life's experiences do not balance out evenly, I am the unsolved remainder. And I know that this remainder, which makes you so frantic, is in reality my love, that you do not yet understand. I am present in your needs. I have suffered them and they are now transformed, but not obliterated from my heart.....This reality — incomprehensible wonder of my almighty love — I have sheltered safely and completely, in the cold stable of your world. I am there. I no longer go away from this world, even if you do not see me now....I am there.'"

Karl Rahner, S.J.

HYMNS

Amazing Grace! How Sweet the Sound

1. A - maz - ing grace! how sweet the
2. 'Twas grace that taught my heart to
3. The Lord has prom - ised good to
4. Through man - y dan - gers, toils, and
5. When we've been there ten thou - sand

sound, That saved a wretch like
fear, And grace my fears re -
me, His word my hope se -
snares, I have al - read - y
years, Bright shin - ing as the

me! I once was
lieved; How pre - cious
cures; He will my
come; 'Tis grace hath
sun, We've no less

lost, but now am found, Was
did that grace ap - pear The
shield and por - tion be As
brought me safe thus far, And
days to sing God's praise Than

blind, but now I see.
hour I first be - lieved!
long as life en - dures.
grace will lead me home.
when we'd first be - gun.

Alleluia! Sing to Jesus

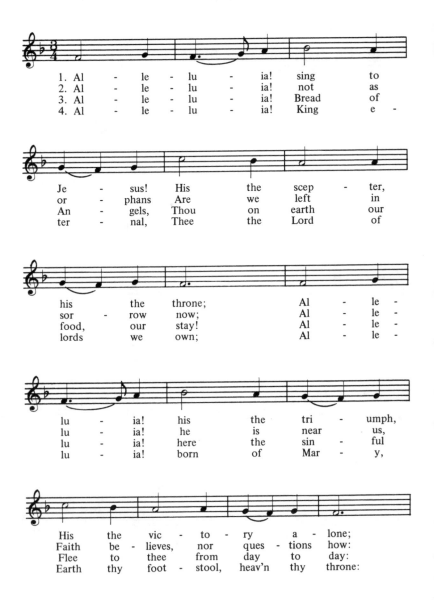

1. Al - le - lu - ia! sing to
2. Al - le - lu - ia! not as
3. Al - le - lu - ia! Bread of
4. Al - le - lu - ia! King e -

Je - sus! His the scep - ter,
or - phans Are we left in
An - gels, Thou on earth our
ter - nal, Thee the Lord of

his the throne; Al - le -
sor - row now; Al - le -
food, our stay! Al - le -
lords we own; Al - le -

lu - ia! his the tri - umph,
lu - ia! he is near us,
lu - ia! here the sin - ful
lu - ia! born of Mar - y,

His the vic - to - ry a - lone;
Faith be - lieves, nor ques - tions how:
Flee to thee from day to day:
Earth thy foot - stool, heav'n thy throne:

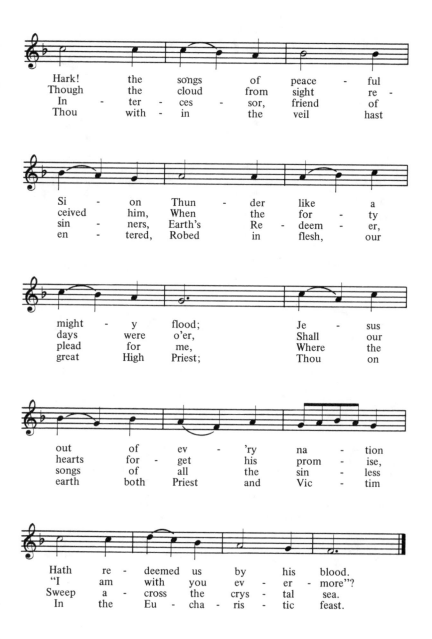

Hark!   the   songs   of   peace -   ful
Though   the   cloud   from sight   re -
In   -   ter - ces - sor, friend   of
Thou   with - in   the   veil   hast

Si   -   on   Thun - der   like   a
ceived   him,   When   the   for   -   ty
sin   -   ners,   Earth's Re - deem -   er,
en   -   tered, Robed   in   flesh,   our

might -   y   flood;   Je   -   sus
days   were   o'er,   Shall   our
plead   for   me,   Where   the
great   High   Priest;   Thou   on

out   of   ev - 'ry   na   -   tion
hearts   for - get   his   prom -   ise,
songs   of   all   the   sin   -   less
earth   both   Priest and   Vic   -   tim

Hath   re -   deemed us   by   his   blood.
"I   am   with   you   ev - er - more"?
Sweep   a   -   cross the   crys - tal sea.
In   the   Eu - cha - ris - tic feast.

A Mighty Fortress

1. A might-y for-tress is our God, A bul-wark nev-er fail - ing,
2. The wa - ters of his good-ness flow Through-out his ho - ly cit - y,
3. Be - hold his won-drous deeds of peace, The God of our sal - va - tion;

1. Pro - tect - ing us with staff and rod, His pow - er all pre - vail - ing.
2. And glad - den hearts of those who know His ten - der - ness and pit - y.
3. He knows our wars and makes them cease In ev - ery land and na - tion.

1. What if the na - tions rage And surg - ing seas ram - page; What though the
2. Though na - tions stand un - sure, God's king-dom shall en - dure; His pow - er
3. The war-rior's spear and lance Are splin-tered by his glance The guns and

1. moun-tains fall, The Lord is God of all; On earth is not his e - qual. 2.
2. shall re - main, His peace shall ev - er reign, Our God, the God of Ja - cob. 3.
3. nu - clear might Stand with-ered in his sight; The Lord of hosts is with us.

At the Cross Her Station Keeping

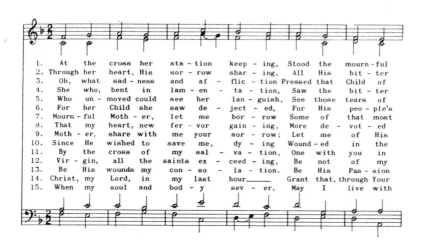

1. At the cross her sta - tion keep - ing, Stood the mourn - ful
2. Through her heart, His sor - row shar - ing, All His bit - ter
3. Oh, what sad - ness and af - flic - tion Pressed that Child of
4. She who, bent in lam - en - ta - tion, Saw the bit - ter
5. Who un - moved could see her lan - guish, See those tears of
6. For her Child she saw de - ject - ed, For His peo - ple's
7. Mourn - ful Moth - er, let me bor - row Some of that most
8. That my heart, new fer - vor gain - ing, More de - vot - ed
9. Moth - er, share with me your sor - row; Let me of His
10. Since He wished to save me, dy - ing Wound - ed in the
11. By the cross of my sal - va - tion, One with you in
12. Vir - gin, all the saints ex - ceed - ing, Be not of my
13. Be His wounds my con - so - la - tion. Be His Pas - sion
14. Christ, my Lord, in my last hour_____ Grant that, through Your
15. When my soul and bod - y sev - er, May I live with

1. Moth - er weep - ing, While her Je - sus hung a - bove.
2. an - guish bear - ing, Ran the sword of suf - f'ring love.
3. ben - e - dic - tion, Moth - er of the Ho - ly One.
4. des - o - la - tion Of her well be - lov - ed Son.
5. bit - ter an - guish stream - ing down her ten - der cheek?
6. sins re - ject - ed, And with blood - y scour - ges rent.
7. bit - ter sor - row, Which for Je - sus you did feel:
8. love at - tain - ing, May to His pierced Heart ap - peal.
9. tor - ments bor - row; Print them on my sin - ful heart.
10. cru - ci - fy - ing, In His suf - f'ring give me part.
11. rep - a - ra - tion, May He all my sins for - give.
12. prayer un - heed - ing; Let me share with you your grief.
13. my sal - va - tion. Be His dy - ing my be - lief.
14. Moth - er's pow - er, I may con - quer ev - 'ry sin.
15. You for - ev - er, To Your glo - ry en - t'ring in.   A - men.

Children Sing with Voice Gay

Chil - dren sing with voi - ces gay, And
wel - come Christ on Christ - mas Day. He
sleeps and smiles, a child so small, Yet
he is King and Lord of all.

2. Angels fill the skies with song
   For him to whom the skies belong.
   They sing of peace on Christmas morn,
   For now the prince of peace is born.

3. Mary sings her lullaby,
   While Joseph stands with watchful eye:
   The shep'herds kneel before their king.
   And kings from far their gifts will bring.

4. Children, sing with voices clear,
   And greet your new-born Saviour dear.
   He is the Lord of heaven above,
   Now born a child to win our love.

The Church's One Foundation

1. The Church's one foun - da - tion Is
2. E - lect from ev - ery na - tion, Yet
3. 'Mid toil and trib - u - la - tion, And
4. Yet she on earth hath un - ion With

Je - sus Christ her Lord; She is his new cre -
one o'er all the earth, Her char - ter of sal -
tu - mult of her war, She waits the con - sum -
God, the Three in One, And mys - tic sweet com -

a - tion By wa - ter and the word;
va - tion, One Lord, one faith, one birth,
ma - tion Of peace for ev - er - more;
mun - ion With those whose rest is won.

From heaven he came and sought her To
One ho - ly name she bless - es, Par -
Till with the vi - sion glo - rious, Her
O hap - py ones and ho - ly! Lord,

be his ho - ly bride; With his own blood he
takes one ho - ly food, And to one hope she
long - ing eyes are blest, And the great Church vic -
give us grace that we Like them, the meek and

bought her, And for her life he died.
press - es, With ev - ery grace en - dued.
to - rious Shall be the Church at rest.
low - ly, On high may dwell with thee. A - men.

Crown Him with Many Crowns

1. Crown	him	with	man -	y	crowns,	The
2. Crown	him	the Lord	of		life,	Who
3. Crown	him	the Lord	of		love,	Be -
4. Crown	him	the Lord	of		peace,	Whose
5. Crown	him	the Lord	of		years,	The

Lamb up - on	his	throne;	Hark!	how the heaven - ly
tri - umphed o'er	the	grave,	And	rose vic - to - rious
hold his hands and		side,	Rich	wounds yet vis - i -
power a scep - tre		sways	From	pole to pole, that
Po - ten - tate of		time,	Cre -	a - tor of the

an - them drowns	All	mu - sic	but	its	own.
in the strife	For	those	he	came to	save.
ble a - bove	In	beau - ty	glo - ri -		fied.
wars may cease,	Ab - sorbed	in	prayer and		praise.
roll - ing spheres,	In - ef - fa -	bly	sub -		lime.

A - wake,	my	soul,	and	sing	Of
His	glo - ries	now	we	sing,	Who
No	an - gel	in	the	sky	Can
His	reign shall	know	no	end,	And
All	hail, Re - deem - er,	hail!	For

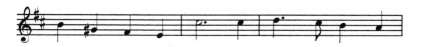

him	who	died	for	thee,	And	hail	him	as	thy
died	and	rose	on	high,	Who	died,	e - ter - nal
ful - ly	bear	that	sight,	But	down - ward bends	his
round	his	pierc - ed	feet	Fair	flowers	of	Par - a -
thou	hast	died	for	me;	Thy	praise	and	glo - ry

match - less	King Through	all	e - ter - ni - ty.
life	to	bring,	And	lives	that	death may	die.
burn - ing	eye	At	mys - ter - ies	so	bright.
dise	ex - tend	Their	fra - grance ev - er	sweet.
shall	not	fail	Through - out	e - ter - ni - ty.

Come Holy Ghost

1. Come Ho - ly Ghost, Cre - a - tor blest,
2. O, Com - fort - er, to thee we cry,
3. O Ho - ly Ghost, Through thee a - lone,
4. Praise we the Lord, Fa - ther and Son,

And in our hearts take up thy rest;
Thou heav'n - ly gift of God Most High;
Know we the Fa - ther and the Son;
And Ho - ly Spir - it with them one;

Come with thy grace and heav'n - ly aid
Thou Fount of Life, and Fire of Love,
Be this our firm un - chang - ing creed,
And may the Son on us be - stow

To fill the hearts which thou hast
And sweet a - noint - ing from a -
That thou dost from them both pro -
All gifts that from the Spir - it

made, To fill the hearts which
bove, And sweet a - noint - ing
ceed, That thou dost from them
flow, All gifts that from the

thou hast made.
from a - bove.
both pro - ceed.
Spir - it flow.   A - men.

Faith of Our Fathers

1. Faith of our fa - thers! liv - ing still
2. Our fa - thers, chained in pris - ons dark,
3. Faith of our fa - thers! faith and prayer
4. Faith of our fa - thers! we will love

In spite of dun - geon, fire, and sword:
Were still in heart and con - science free:
Shall win all na - tions un - to thee;
Both friend and foe in all our strife:

O how our hearts beat high with joy,
And tru - ly blest would be our fate,
And through the truth that comes from God,
And preach thee, too, as loves knows how,

When - e'er we hear that glo - rious word:
If we, like them, should die for thee.
Man - kind shall then in - deed be free.
By kind - ly deeds and vir - tuous life.

Faith of our fa - thers, ho - ly faith!

We will be true to thee till death.

God's Blessing Sends Us Forth

God's bless - ing sends us forth,

Strength - ened for our task on earth,

Re - freshed in soul, re - newed in mind.

May God with us re - main, Through us his

Spi - rit reign That Christ be known to all man -

kind.

2. God's news in spoken word
   Joyfully our hearts have heard;
   O may the seed of God's love now grow.
   May we in fruitful deeds
   Gladly serve others' needs
   That faith in action we may show.

3. We by one living bread
   As one body have been fed,
   So we are one in true brotherhood;
   How gracious to behold
   All brethren of one fold
   Who ever seek each other's good.

Hail Queen of Heaven

Hail, Queen of heav'n, the o - cean star,

Guide of the wan - d'rer here be - low: Thrown

on life's surge, we claim thy care: Save us from

pe - ril and from woe. Mo - ther of Christ,

star of the sea, Pray for the wan - d'rer,

pray for me.

2. O gentle, chaste and spotless maid,
We sinners make our prayers through thee:
Remind thy Son that he has paid
The price of our iniquity.
Virgin most pure, star of the sea,
Pray for the sinner, pray for me.

How Great Thou Art

1. O Lord my God! When I in awesome wonder consider all the *worlds thy hands have made, I see the stars, I hear the *rolling thunder, thy pow'r throughout the universe displayed,
   Then sings my soul, my Savior God to thee; how great thou art!
   Then sings my soul, my Savior God to thee; how great thou art, how great thou art!
2. When through the woods and forest glades I wander and hear the birds sing sweetly in the trees;
   When I look down from loftly mountain grandeur and hear the brook and feel the gentle breeze;
3. And when I think that God, his Son not sparing, sent him to die, I scarce can take it in;
   That on the cross, my burden gladly bearing, he bled and died to take away my sin;
4. When Christ shall come with shout of acclamation and take me home, what joy shall fill my heart!
   Then I shall bow in humble adoration and there proclaim, my God, how great thou art!

I Am the Bread of Life

S. Suzanne Toolan, 1970

Let Us Break Bread Together

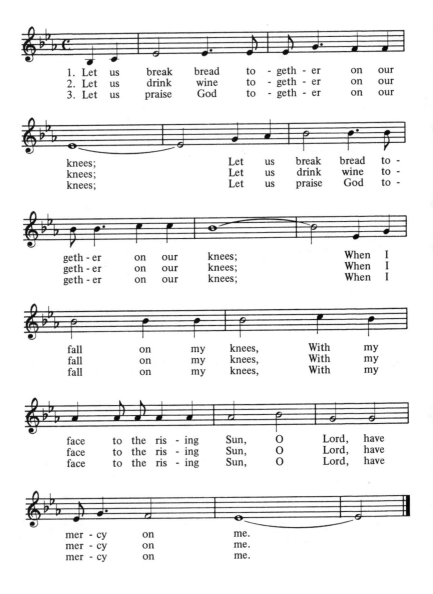

The Magnificat

Sung to the Melody of Amazing Grace

My soul proclaims the Lord my God
My spirit sings His praise!
He looks on me, He lifts me up,
And gladness fills my days.

All nations now will share my joy,
His gifts He has outpoured,
His little ones He has made great,
I magnify the Lord.

His mercy is for everymore!
His name I praise again.
His strong right arm puts down the proud
And raises lowly ones.

He fills the hungry with good things,
The rich He sends away.
The promise made to Abraham
is filled by Him each day.

Magnificat, Magnificat!
Magnificat, bless God!
Magnificat, Magnificat,
Magnificat, bless God!

O Come, O Come, Emmanuel

1. O	come,	O	come, Em -	man		u -	el,
2. O	come,	Thou	Wis - dom,	from		on	high,
3. O	come,	O	come, Thou	Lord		of	might,
4. O	come,	Thou	rod	of	Jes -	se's	stem,
5. O	come,	Thou	key	of	Dav -	id,	come,
6. O	come,	Thou	Day - spring	from		on	high
7. O	come,	De -	sire	of	na -	tions,	bind

And	ran -	som	cap - tive	Is -		ra -	el,
Who	ord -	'rest	all	things	migh -	ti -	ly;
Who	to	Thy	tribes	on	Si -	nai's	height
From	ev -	'ry	foe	de - li -		ver	them
And	o -	pen	wide	our	heav'n -	ly	home;
And	cheer	us	by	Thy	draw -	ing	nigh;
In	one	the	hearts	of	all	man -	kind;

That	mourns	in	lone - ly	ex -		ile	here
To	us	the	path	of	knowl -	edge	show,
In	an -	cient	times	didst	give	the	law,
That	trust	Thy	might - y	power		to	save,
Make	safe	the	way	that	leads	on	high,
Dis -	perse	the	gloom - y	clouds		of	night,
Bid	Thou	our	sad	di - vi -		sions	cease,

Un - til	the	Son	of	God		ap -	pear.
And teach	us	in	her	ways		to	go.
In cloud,	and	ma - jes -	ty,			and	awe.
And give	them	vict - 'ry	o'er			the	grave.
And close	the	path	to	mis -		er -	y.
And death's	dark	shad - ow	put			to	flight.
And be	Thy - self	our	King			of	Peace.

Re - joice!	Re - joice!	Em -	man -		u -	el

Shall	come	to	Thee,	O	Is -	ra -	el!

Sacred Head Surrounded

O sa - cred head sur - round - ed By crown of pierc - ing thorn. O bleed - ing head so wound - ed, Re - viled and put to scorn. Our sins have marred the glo - ry Of thy most ho - ly face. Yet an - gel hosts a - dore thee, And trem - ble as they gaze.

2. The Lord of every nation
   Was hung upon a tree;
   His death was our salvation,
   Our sins, his agony.
   O Jesus, by thy Passion,
   Thy life in us increase;
   Thy death for us did fashion
   Our pardon and our peace.

Priestly People

Priest - ly peo - ple, King - ly peo - ple, Ho - ly peo - ple,

God's cho - sen peo - ple, Sing praise to the Lord.

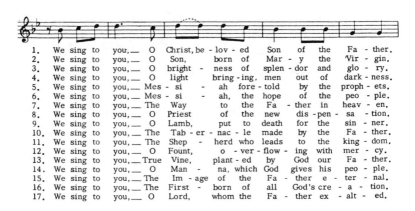

1. We sing to you,— O Christ, be - lov - ed Son of the Fa - ther.
2. We sing to you,— O Son, born of Mar - y the Vir - gin.
3. We sing to you,— O bright - ness of splen - dor and glo - ry.
4. We sing to you,— O light bring - ing, men out of dark - ness.
5. We sing to you,— Mes - si - ah fore - told by the proph - ets.
6. We sing to you,— Mes - si - ah, the hope of the peo - ple.
7. We sing to you,— The Way to the Fa - ther in heav - en.
8. We sing to you,— O Priest of the new dis - pen - sa - tion.
9. We sing to you,— O Lamb, put to death for the sin - ner.
10. We sing to you,— The Tab - er - nac - le made by the Fa - ther.
11. We sing to you,— The Shep - herd who leads to the king - dom.
12. We sing to you,— O Fount, o - ver - flow - ing with mer - cy.
13. We sing to you,—True Vine, plant - ed by God our Fa - ther.
14. We sing to you,— O Man - na, which God gives his peo - ple.
15. We sing to you,— The Im - age of the Fa - ther e - ter - nal.
16. We sing to you,— The First - born of all God's cre - a - tion.
17. We sing to you,— O Lord, whom the Fa - ther ex - alt - ed.

1. We give you praise, O Wis - dom ev - er - last - ing, and Word of God.
2. We give you praise, Our Broth - er, born to heal us, our sav - ing Lord.
3. We give you praise, O Morn - ing Star, an - nounc -ing the com - ing day.
4. We give you praise, O guid - ing Light, who shows us the way to heaven.
5. We give you praise, O Son of Da - vid and Son of A - bra - ham.
6. We give you praise, O Christ, our Lord and King, hum - ble, meek of heart.
7. We give you praise, The Way of Truth, and Way of all grace and light.
8. We give you praise, Our Peace, sealed by the blood of the Sac - ri - fice.
9. We give you praise, O Vic - tim, im - mo - lat - ed for all man - kind.
10. We give you praise, The Cor - ner -stone and Sav -ior of Is - ra - el.
11. We give you praise, Who gath - er all your sheep in the one true fold.
12. We give you praise, Who give us liv - ing wa -ters to quench our thirst
13. We give you praise, O bless - ed Vine, whose branch -es bear fruit in love.
14. We give you praise, O liv - ing Bread, which comes down to us from heaven
15. We give you praise, O King of jus - tice, Lord, and the King of peace
16. We give you praise, Sal - va - tion of your saints sleep -ing in the Lord.
17. We give you praise, In glo - ry you are com - ing to judge all men.

Sing of Mary

1. Sing of Ma - ry, pure and low - ly,
2. Sing of Je - sus, son of Ma - ry,
3. Glo - ry be to God the Fa - ther;

Vir - gin - moth - er un - de - filed,
In the home at Na - za - reth.
Glo - ry be to God the Son;

Sing of God's own Son most ho - ly,
Toil and la - bor can - not wea - ry
Glo - ry be to God the Spir - it;

Who be - came her lit - tle child.
Love en - dur - ing un - to death.
Glo - ry to the Three in One.

Fair - est	child	of	fair - est	moth - er,
Con - stant	was	the	love	he	gave	her,
From	the	heart	of	bless - ed	Ma - ry,

God	the	Lord	who	came	to	earth,
Though	he	went	forth	from	her	side,
From	all	saints	the	song	as - cends,

Word	made	flesh,	our	ver - y	broth - er,
Forth	to	preach,	and	heal,	and	suf - fer,
And	the	Church	the	strain	re - ec - hoes

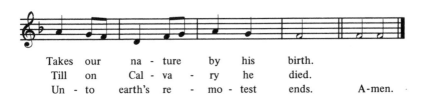

Takes	our	na - ture	by	his	birth.
Till	on	Cal - va - ry	he	died.
Un - to	earth's	re - mo - test	ends.	A - men.

The Spirit of God

The Spir-it of God rests up-on me,___ The Spir-it of God con-se-crates me,___ The Spir-it of God bids me go forth to pro-claim his peace, his joy.

1. The Spir - it of God sends me forth, Called to wit - ness the king-dom of Christ a - mong all the na - tions;
2. The Spir - it of God sends me forth, Called to wit - ness the king-dom of Christ a - mong all the na - tions;
3. The Spir - it of God sends me forth, Called to wit - ness the king-dom of Christ a - mong all the na - tions;
4. The Spir - it of God sends me forth, Called to wit - ness the king-dom of Christ a - mong all the na - tions;
5. The Spir - it of God sends me forth, Called to wit - ness the king-dom of Christ a - mong all the na - tions;

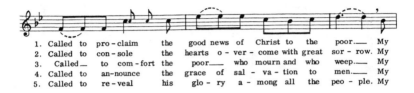

1. Called to pro-claim the good news of Christ to the poor.___ My
2. Called to con-sole the hearts o - ver - come with great sor - row. My
3. Called___ to com-fort the poor___ who mourn and who weep.___ My
4. Called to an-nounce the grace of sal - va - tion to men.___ My
5. Called to re-veal his glo - ry a - mong all the peo - ple. My

Repeat Antiphon

1. spir - it re - joic - es in God, my Sav - ior.
2. spir - it re - joic - es in God, my Sav - ior.
3. spir - it re - joic - es in God, my Sav - ior.
4. spir - it re - joic - es in God, my Sav - ior.
5. spir - it re - joic - es in God, my Sav - ior.

There Is One Lord

There is one ___ Lord, there is one ___ faith, there is one ___ bap - tism, one God, who is Fa - ther.

1. We were called to be one in the Spir - it of God, in the bond of peace, We sing and ___ we pro-claim. *Antiphon*

2. We were called to form one bod - y in one spir - it, We sing and ___ we pro-claim. *Antiphon*

3. We were called in the same hope in ___ Christ the Lord, We sing and ___ we pro- claim. *Antiphon*

The Holy City

Last night I lay asleeping
　there came a dream so fair
I stood in old Jerusalem beside
　the temple there
I heard the children singing
　and ever as they sang
Methought the voice of Angels
　from heaven in answer rang
Methought the voice of Angels
　from heaven in answer rang.

Refrain:　Jerusalem Jerusalem lift up your gates and sing
　　　　　hosanna in the highest
　　　　　hosanna to your king.

Then suddenly the scene was changed.
　the streets no longer rang
Hushed were the glad hosannas
　the little children sang
The earth grew dark with
　mystery, the morn was cold and chill
　as the shadow of a cross arose
　upon a lonely hill
　as the shadow of a cross arose
　upon a lonely hill. (Refrain)

And then the scene was changed again
　new earth there seemed to be.
I saw the Holy City beside the
　tideless sea
The light of God was on its streets,
　the gates were open wide
And all who would might enter
　and no one denied
No need of moon or stars by night
　or sun to shine by day
It was the new Jerusalem that
　would not pass away. (Refrain)

We Three Kings of Orient Are

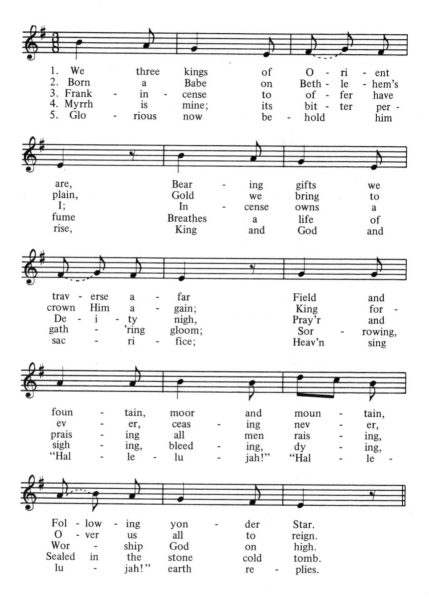

1. We three kings of Orient are,
2. Born a Babe on Bethlehem's
3. Frank - in - cense to of - fer have
4. Myrrh is mine; its bit - ter per -
5. Glo - rious now be - hold him

are, Bear - ing gifts we
plain, Gold we bring to
I; In - cense owns a
fume Breathes a life of
rise, King and God and

trav - erse a - far Field and
crown Him a - gain; King for -
De - i - ty nigh, Pray'r and
gath - 'ring gloom; Sor - rowing,
sac - ri - fice; Heav'n sing

foun - tain, moor and moun - tain,
ev - er, ceas - ing nev - er,
prais - ing all men rais - ing,
sigh - ing, bleed - ing, dy - ing,
"Hal - le - lu - jah!" "Hal - le -

Fol - low - ing yon - der Star.
O - ver us all to reign.
Wor - ship God on high.
Sealed in the stone cold tomb.
lu - jah!" earth re - plies.

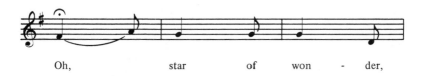

Oh,   star   of   won - der,

star   of   night,   Star   with

roy - al   beau - ty   bright,

West - ward   lead - ing,   still   pro - ceed - ing,

Guide   us   to   the   per - fect   Light.

Were You There?

1. Were you there when they cru - ci - fied my
2. Were you there when they nailed him to the
3. Were you there when they laid him in the
4. Were you there when they rolled the stone a -

Lord? Were you there when they
tree? Were you there when they
tomb? Were you there when they
way? Were you there when they

[⌢]   [⌢]

cru - ci - fied my Lord? Oh!
nailed him to the tree? Oh!
laid him in the tomb? Oh!
rolled the stone a - way? Oh!

Some - times it caus - es me to trem - ble,
Some - times it caus - es me to trem - ble,
Some - times it caus - es me to trem - ble,
Some - times it caus - es me to trem - ble,

[⌢]

trem - ble, trem - ble. Were you there when they
trem - ble, trem - ble. Were you there when they
trem - ble, trem - ble. Were you there when they
trem - ble, trem - ble. Were you there when they

cru - ci - fied my Lord?
nailed him to the tree?
laid him in the tomb?
rolled the stone a - way?

Whatsoever You Do

What-so - ev - er you do to the least of my

broth-ers, that you do un - to me.

1. When I was hun - gry, you gave me to eat;
2. When I was home- less, you o - pened your door;
3. When I was wea - ry, you helped me find rest;
4. When I was lit - tle, you taught me to read;
5. When in a pris - on, you came to my cell;
6. In a strange coun - try, you made me at home;
7. Hurt in a bat - tle, you bound up my wounds;
8. When I was Ne - gro, or Chi - nese, or white;
9. When I was a - ged, you both - ered to smile;
10. You saw me cov - ered with spit - tle and blood;
11. When I was laughed at, you stood by my side;

When I was thirst - y, you gave me to drink.
When I was na - ked, you gave me your coat.
When I was anx - ious, you calmed all my fears.
When I was lone - ly, you gave me your love.
When on a sick bed, you cared for my needs.
Seek - ing em - ploy - ment, you found me a job.
Search - ing for kind - ness, you held out your hand.
Mocked and in - sult - ed, you car - ried my cross.
When I was rest - less, you lis - tened and cared.
You knew my fea - tures, though grim - y with sweat.
When I was hap - py, you shared in my joy.

Now en - ter in - to the home of my Fa - ther.

Where Charity and Love Prevail

1. Where char - i - ty and love pre - vail
2. With grate - ful joy and ho - ly fear
3. For - give we now each oth - er's faults
4. Let strife a - mong us be un - known,
5. Let us re - call that in our midst
6. No race nor creed can love ex - clude

1. There God is ev - er found;
2. His char - i - ty we learn;
3. As we our faults con - fess;
4. Let all con - ten - tion cease;
5. Dwells God's be - got - ten Son;
6. If hon - ored be God's Name;

1. Brought here to - geth - er by Christ's love
2. Let us with heart and mind and soul
3. And let us love each oth - er well
4. Be his the glo - ry that we seek,
5. As mem - bers of his Bod - y joined
6. Our broth - er - hood em - brac - es all

1. By love are we thus bound.
2. Now love him in re - turn.
3. In Chris - tian ho - li - ness.
4. Be ours his ho - ly peace.
5. We are in him made one.
6. Whose Fa - ther is the same.

Yes, I Shall Arise

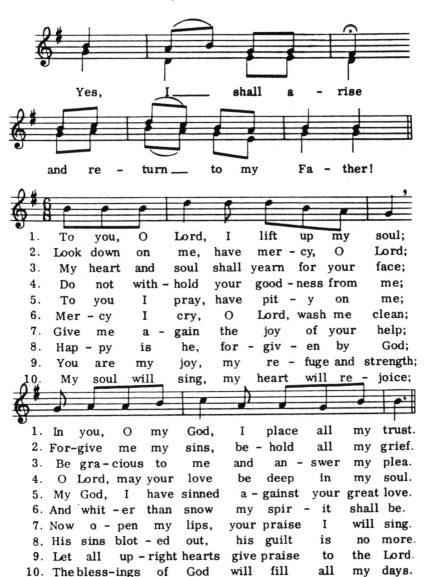

Yes, I shall a - rise and re - turn to my Fa - ther!

1. To you, O Lord, I lift up my soul;
2. Look down on me, have mer - cy, O Lord;
3. My heart and soul shall yearn for your face;
4. Do not with - hold your good - ness from me;
5. To you I pray, have pit - y on me;
6. Mer - cy I cry, O Lord, wash me clean;
7. Give me a - gain the joy of your help;
8. Hap - py is he, for - giv - en by God;
9. You are my joy, my re - fuge and strength;
10. My soul will sing, my heart will re - joice;

1. In you, O my God, I place all my trust.
2. For-give me my sins, be - hold all my grief.
3. Be gra - cious to me and an - swer my plea.
4. O Lord, may your love be deep in my soul.
5. My God, I have sinned a - gainst your great love.
6. And whit - er than snow my spir - it shall be.
7. Now o - pen my lips, your praise I will sing.
8. His sins blot - ed out, his guilt is no more.
9. Let all up - right hearts give praise to the Lord.
10. The bless-ings of God will fill all my days.

Silent Night

1. Si - lent night, ho - ly night,
2. Si - lent night, ho - ly night,
3. Si - lent night, ho - ly night,

All is calm, all is bright
Shep - herds quake at the sight;
Son of God, love's pure light

Round yon Vir - gin Moth - er and Child.
Glo - ries stream from heav - en a - far,
Ra - diant beams from thy ho - ly face,

Ho - ly In - fant, so ten - der and mild,
Heaven - ly hosts sing, Al - le - lu - ia,
With the dawn of re - deem - ing grace,

Sleep in heav - en - ly peace,
Christ, the Sav - iour, is born!
Je - sus, Lord, at thy birth.

Sleep in heav - en - ly peace.
Christ, the Sav - iour, is born!
Je - sus, Lord, at thy birth.

O Come, All Ye Faithful

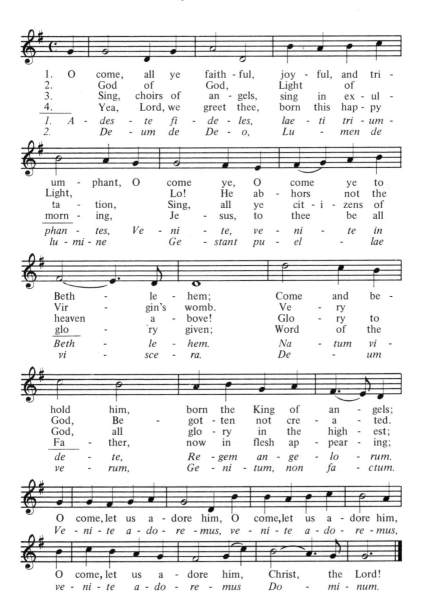

1. O come, all ye faith-ful, joy-ful, and tri-um-phant, O come ye, O come ye to Beth - le - hem; Come and be-hold him, born the King of an - gels;
2. God of God, Light of Light, Lo! He ab-hors not the Vir - gin's womb. Ve - ry God, Be-got - ten not cre - a - ted.
3. Sing, choirs of an - gels, sing in ex-ul-ta - tion, Sing, all ye cit-i-zens of heaven a - bove! Glo - ry to God, all glo - ry in the high - est;
4. Yea, Lord, we greet thee, born this hap-py morn - ing, Je - sus, to thee be all glo - ry given; Word of the Fa - ther, now in flesh ap - pear - ing;

1. *A - des - te fi - de - les, lae - ti tri - um - phan - tes, Ve - ni - te, ve - ni - te in Beth - le - hem. Na - tum vi - de - te, Re - gem an - ge - lo - rum.*
2. *De - um de De - o, Lu - men de lu - mi - ne Ge - stant pu - el - lae vi - sce - ra. De - um ve - rum, Ge - ni - tum, non fa - ctum.*

O come, let us a - dore him, O come, let us a - dore him,
O come, let us a - dore him, Christ, the Lord!

Ve - ni - te a - do - re - mus, ve - ni - te a - do - re - mus,
ve - ni - te a - do - re - mus Do - mi - num.

Angels We Have Heard on High

1. Angels we have heard on high
Sweetly singing o'er the plains, And the mountains in
reply echoing their joyous strain.
Gloria in excelsis Deo
Gloria in excelsis Deo

2. Shepherds, why this jubilee
Why your joyous strains prolong?
What the gladsome tiding be,
Which inspire your joyous song.
Gloria in excelsis Deo.
Gloria in excelsis Deo.

Holy, Holy, Holy! Lord God Almighty

1. Holy, holy, holy! Lord God Almighty! Early in the morning
our song shall rise to thee: Holy, holy, holy! Merciful and
mighty, God in three persons, blessed Trinity.
2. Holy, holy, holy! Though the darkness hide thee, Though
the eye of sinful man thy glory may not see, Only thou art
holy; there is none beside thee, Perfect in power, in love, and
purity.
3. Holy, holy, holy! Lord God Almighty! All thy works shall
praise thy name in earth, and sky, and sea; Holy, holy, holy!
Merciful and mighty, God in three persons, blessed Trinity.

Michael Row the Boat Ashore

Michael row the boat ashore
Alleluia
Michael row the boat ashore,
Alleluia

River Jordan is chilly and cold,
Alleluia
Chills the body but not the soul,
Alleluia
refrain

River Jordan is deep and wide
Alleluia
Got my home on the other side
Alleluia

Swing Low

Swing low, sweet chariot,
comin for to carry me home
Swing low, sweet chariot,
comin for to carry me home

I looked over Jordan and what did I see
comin for to carry me home?
A band of angels comin after me,
comin for to carry me home.

refrain

Battle Hymn of the Republic

1. Mine eyes have seen the glory of the coming of the Lord:
   He is trampling out the vintage where the grapes of
      wrath are stored:
   He hath loosed the fateful lightning of his terrible swift sword:
   His truth is marching on,
   Glory, glory, Hallelujah!
   Glory, glory, Hallelujah!
   Glory, glory, Hallelujah!
   His truth is Marching on.

2. In the beauty of the lilies Christ was born across the sea.
   With a glory in his bosom that transfigures you and me;
   As he died to make men holy, let us die to make men free,
   While God is marching on.
   Glory, glory, Hallelujah!
   Glory, glory, Hallelujah!
   Glory, glory, Hallelujah!
   His truth is marching on.

For All the Saints

1. For all the saints, who from their labors rest, Who you by faith before the world confessed, Your name, O Jesus, be for ever blest. Alleluia, alleluia.

2. You were their rock, their fortress, and their might: You, Lord, their Captain in the well-fought fight; And, in the darkness drear, the one true light. Alleluia, alleluia.

3. O may your soldiers, faithful, true, and bold, Fight as the saints who nobly fought of old, And win, with them, the victor's crown of gold. Alleluia, alleluia.

NOTES

ABOUT THE AUTHOR

Stephen C. Doyle, O.F.M., is Professor of Sacred Scripture and Biblical Preaching at Pope John XXIII National Seminary in Weston, Massachusetts. He has been teaching the Bible for twenty years, including courses in Biblical Archaeology and Geography. He has also led over twenty-five groups on retreat-study pilgrimages to the Holy Land. His publications include: *Covenant Renewal in Religious Life; Prayers for a New Day;* and *The Gospel in Word and Power.*

INDEX

215